for World Revolution

by

El Lissitzky

Translated by Eric Dluhosch

The M.I.T. Press
Massachusetts Institute of Technology
Cambridge, Massachusetts

First MIT Press paperback edition, 1984

Originally published in 1930 by Verlag Anton Schroll & Co., Vienna, under the title "Rußland, Die Rekonstruktion der Architektur in der Sowjetunion." Second edition published in 1965 by Ullstein Verlag, under the title "Rußland: Architektur für eine Weltrevolution"

English translation copyright © 1970 by The Massachusetts Institute of Technology

Library of Congress catalog card number: 70-92782

ISBN 0-262-62047-2 (paperback)

Printed and bound in the United States of America

Russia: An Architecture for World Revolution

Translator's Preface

New ideas and new directions in art never "just happen." They only seem to enter the public mind as something sudden and unexpected, for in reality no artistic movement has ever emerged "out of nothing." Present, so-called "avant-garde" art production is no exception. Most contemporary art movements have their roots in the twenties of this century. The rediscovery of El Lissitzky is therefore neither accidental nor a matter of mere historical sentimentality. Lissitzky is to contemporary art production what Charles Babbage was to computer technology in 1819. Just as the then existing machine-tool technology was incapable of translating Babbage's plans for the "analytical machine" into reality, so were the means of the artist in 1920 insufficient to create stereophonic effects, light shows, holographs, and so on (an example in the text shows the impossibility of completely realizing the design of El Lissitzky's electromechanical show *Victory Over the Sun*).

Another factor of vital importance is the meeting between an idea and the public. Enthusiastic individuals and open-minded institutions are needed to accomplish the task of transmitting information.

Thus, it seems appropriate at this point to acknowledge the help of those institutions and individuals who have made this effort possible. I came across the original text during some research work in Russian city planning at Cornell University. To my great surprise, no English translation of this important book existed at the time. Later I became sufficiently fascinated by the work of Lissitzky to translate the text in its entirety.

Correspondence with the German publisher, Anton Schroll Verlag, confirmed the nonexistence of an English version and also led to an eventual exchange of letters between myself and Mrs. Sophie Lissitzky, who is presently living in Novosibirsk. She was at that time completing El Lissitzky's biography, mentioned in the text. She kindly gave her permission for the translation and publication of El Lissitzky's *Russia: An Architecture for World Revolution*, in the United States, joyful that her late husband's work would finally become more widely known in the English-speaking world. Apart from bringing this book before the American public, this event must surely represent a great—even though late—gift to Sophie Lissitzky, who fought untiringly for decades to publicize and sustain the spirit of her husband's work both during his lifetime and after his tragic death.

Still, all the above would have been in vain without the help and enthusiasm of The MIT Press, especially in the persons of Michael Connolly and Joseph

Stein, whose encouragement and professional skill have made it possible to complete this labor of love and have it published now. I should also like to acknowledge my debt to Mr. Anatole Senkevitch, Jr., for information on the evolution of professional societies in Russia.

Very special thanks are due to Mrs. Fannia Weingartner, not only for her expert advice and for giving the translation its final polish, but also for editing with her heart, thus bringing to the task more than just better grammar and syntax.

Ultimately, the real moving force behind this wonderful book is the fresh and honest humanity of El Lissitzky himself—a matter to be discovered by the reader with the first page of Lissitzky's own writing.

University of California
Berkeley, California
November 17, 1969   Eric Dluhosch

Contents

List of Illustrations in Text

entitled "Floating Object." Direct light was subdued by cloth wall coverings, and the lower part of the window was shaded by adjustable louvres which could be opened or closed for different light effects.

Fig. 35. El Lissitzky: Exhibition space with vertical wood slats.
Fig. 36. Babenkov, Vlassov, and Poliakov: Sketch of the general plan for a new Socialist city near Novosibirsk.
Fig. 37. Plan of a so-called "quarter" in the city of Shcheglovsk.
Fig. 38. General plan of the city of Magnitogorsk.
Fig. 39. General plan of the city of Tirgan.

List of Plates

Preface to the Revised Edition of 1965

Ulrich Conrads has requested me to write a preface to the new (old) book, El Lissitzky's *Russia*, which originally appeared in 1930 as part of the series "New Construction in the World," published by Joseph Gantner. He did so because of my close association with Lissitzky from 1934 to 1937, the last years of my stay in Moscow prior to my arrest and banishment from the Soviet Union.

Much that is personal inevitably intrudes into an undertaking of this kind. This often happens when I am asked to write about old friends who have died recently or long ago. Some of my present, younger friends frequently ask me: "How was it possible for you, a budding young architect, to become so intimate with so many of the well-known great 'innovators' during the 1920's despite the fact that they were all much older than you?"

There was indeed an *International* of the spirit which at that time sympathetically drew us younger members into its circle. It survived all the commotion of the 1930's and of the Second World War, and at the same time saved our generation from becoming more or less enthusiastic fellow travelers of Fascism.

El Lissitzky was born in Vitebsk, that singular—one might almost say mysterious—Jewish community whose ambience has been immortalized in innumerable paintings of all kinds of living creatures, from people to donkeys, by Marc Chagall, Lissitzky's friend and fellow student. Chagall, who was born at approximately the same time as Lissitzky, survives him.

Lissitzky became known to us in Germany during the 1920's while he was designing exhibits sponsored by the new Soviet state in other countries. In the process, perhaps unconsciously, he opened up entirely new paths for architectural forms, transcending by far his completely new and revolutionary technique for mounting exhibits. He rapidly established communication with all of the progressive elements in Germany.

In Hanover he became acquainted with Sophie Küppers, widow of the director of the Kestner Society, took her and her two sons to Moscow and there married her. There, regardless of all the racial and physical differences (he suffered from tuberculosis at an early age), they led a very happy married existence and had another son, his beloved Bubka, who developed into a healthy and well-adjusted young man despite his hereditary disadvantages. Lissitzky created an atmosphere of love for his entire family, above all his "little Sophie," and he supplied them with whatever luxury was possible in the new Russia. He protected them against all adversity and the envy of his whole tribe—I almost said *Mishpochah*—and built, as it were, a pedestal for his beautiful wife, on whom he squandered all the resources at his disposal.

For the most part he lived in *dachas* (wooden huts) on the outskirts of Moscow and was happiest in the circle of his large family and his friends. These included, above all, my brother-in-law, Hans Leistikov, and his wife; Hans Schmidt and his wife; and Mr. and Mrs. Schutte-Lihotsky. Among his friends, until their death, were the two brothers Vesnin, as well as Ladovski, Ginsburg, and Leonidov, all architects, and also such men as Malevich, Melnikov, Mayakovsky, Meyerhold, Pudovkin, Dsiga Werthoff, and many others. Here was, in short, the entire élite of new Russia, attempting to work out a new future for all artistic endeavors in the course of endless discussions.

When Stalin's "Socialist realism" began to take effect, life became gradually more lonesome for Lissitzky. His circle shrank as a result of arrests and, in the case of foreigners, deportations. Many of the "survivors" no longer dared remain in contact with us, and the very last more or less festive gatherings were limited to Lissitzky's and my own immediate families.

It was a cruel fate for El Lissitzky to live to see all his grandiose ideas of the 1920's—which are documented in this book and in part remain surprisingly timely—disgraced and practically eradicated. But he persisted in trying to discover the ideological reason for this total reversal of all cultural life, even though he himself had been one of the outstanding pioneers of the so-called functionalism. This was far more tragic for him than for me, his junior in age, who had in the year 1930 just constructed the new tuberculosis sanatorium *Sonnenblick* in Marburg. At that time, on my departure for Moscow in the company of Ernst May, the *Oberhessische Zeitung* commented: "There at last goes the Jewish Bolshevik where he belongs." Two years later, in Moscow, I was to hear myself called a capitalistic functionalist. How often did the two of us discuss these peculiar metamorphoses— the Soviet functionalist Jew El Lissitzky and the German functionalist Aryan Hebebrand!

And then, one day, my hour struck: arrest in December, 1937, and deportation to Germany directly from prison in May of 1938. We had foreseen what was coming: during those last days we sent my little son Karl to the Lissitzkys to spare him from witnessing it all. He was playing unconcernedly with his little friend Bubka at the time the GPU came to arrest me in the middle of the night. It was Lissitzky who advised my despairing wife to depart for Germany immediately on the only possible grounds that: here you can do nothing toward his liberation; it might perhaps be better in Fascist Germany. He consoled her, and, after the last bottle of champagne was gone, he gave her three wine goblets from his old, prerevolutionary possessions. These have in the meantime reached my son's family in the United States, where today they are used to drink toasts to new grandchildren and on all other family occasions.

I have never seen Sophie Lissitzky since. After her husband's death, ill fortune befell her. She now lives in Novosibirsk. I am told that after the war she paid two brief visits to Vienna and there declared to our friends that she did not ever want to return to Europe. One of the sons from her first marriage later returned to Germany and is no longer alive; the second son and Bubka live in the Soviet Union.

For us few survivors of the old circle of intimates, both the artist and the man El Lissitzky will remain unforgettable. He is one of the people who contributed to the formation of my philosophy of life. I am thankful and happy to have been one of his friends.

Hamburg
Spring 1965   Werner Hebebrand

Translator's Introduction

Evaluation or interpretation, or both, make up most introductions. I shall try to avoid this pattern, and instead make an attempt to complement the main text with a few additional facts and dates.

The Appendix extends the text, recounting the events that superseded Lissitzky's activities and describing the developments that led from the brief era of "Communist heroism" to the dark period of "Socialist realism." A cursory excursion back into history and a brief outline of Russian architecture prior to the time of Lissitzky's activities seem necessary prerequisites for a deeper understanding of the whole subject.

Before I launch into history, a few remarks concerning Lissitzky himself are in order. The biography in Part I of the Appendix is very short and somewhat incomplete. The exact date of his birth is November 23 (according to the old Russian calendar, November 10), 1890. He was born in Polshinok, a small town near Smolensk. In one of his letters to Sophie Küppers, later to become his wife, Lissitzky wrote, "So you see I don't really know when I was born, and it doesn't matter at all whether I know or not. It serves no purpose to work out a timetable of one's life, as the end cannot be known."[1]

His childhood was spent in an orthodox Jewish milieu. In fact, had it not been for his mother's intransigence, he might have become an American, for his father spent some time in the United States as an immigrant and returned to Russia only after his wife refused to join him in the New World. Lissitzky's frequent references to American conditions may be seen as reflections of his father's experiences in that country. His father was well educated and well traveled. He spoke Russian, Yiddish, German, and English, and in his spare time translated Heine and Shakespeare into Russian. Clearly, Lissitzky's background was not proletarian. After his return from the USA, young Eleazar's father took over the management of an agency for a glass and porcelain factory in Vitebsk.

The other great influence on Lissitzky's life was his German education and the many years he spent in Western Europe. Out of the fifty-one years of his life, Lissitzky spent approximately ten years

---

[1] Sophie Lissitzky-Küppers, *El Lissitzky* (Greenwich, Connecticut: New York Graphic Society, 1968), p. 54.

abroad. In 1922 he met Sophie Küppers in Hanover, where she ran a gallery and, exhibited among other works, Lissitzky's Prouns. She later became his mentor and friend, and eventually accompanied him to Russia where they were married on January 27, 1925. Sophie Lissitzky has survived her husband and at present lives in Novosibirsk. Her recent book, *El Lissitzky* (originally published in German by the Verlag der Kunst in Dresden, in 1967), is a moving testimonial to her husband's work as well as a monument to her own devotion to him and to her strength of character.

In her book, Sophie recalls the young Lissitzky as "a small, slender, slightly stooping figure . . . I looked into fascinating dark eyes, which shone out at me from under a splendid forehead . . . He was touchingly easy to please, and totally impractical in everything which did not directly concern his work . . ."[2] In 1924 Lissitzky's right lung collapsed. Fragile health, years of hard work, and complete obliviousness to material things had taken their toll. When he became fully aware of his physical condition, he contemplated suicide. Only Sophie's loyalty and friendship and his deep-rooted tenacity prevented this disaster. He spent two years in Switzerland recovering his health. But even such serious illness did not halt his wide-ranging creative activities. A stream of letters kept coming and going; to cover medical expenses he did some commercial art work for the German ink concern Pelikan; he cooperated with Hans Arp on the publication of *Kunstismen ;* he wrote articles, experimented with photograms, and so on. Anyone interested in this period of Lissitzky's life should not fail to read the letters published in Sophie's book.

One might ask why recognition of this man's greatness and importance has been so long in coming. Certainly his basic modesty must be seen as one of the reasons for the relative silence that has surrounded his name since his death. From letters, publications, credits, and other material, it is obvious that Lissitzky was on friendly terms with most of the pioneers of the modern movement in architecture, including Grosz, Van Doesburg, Oud, Huszar, van Eesteren, Vantongerloo, Mies van der Rohe, Matthew Josephson, Laszlo Moholy-Nagy, Raoul Hausman, Hans Richter, Werner Gräff, Kurt Schwitters, Hans Arp, Walter Gropius, Bruno Taut, and so on. All these names are well known both to architects and to the art-loving public in the West.

---

[2] *Op. cit.*, p. 101.

Each of these men contributed to modern architecture, and many succeeded beyond the limits of their most ambitious dreams. In fact, they have come to represent the new "academy" in the West. That Lissitzky is not among them is due to his dedication to Socialism, a dedication that he demonstrated by returning to Russia so as to devote all his energies to the realization of his ideas.

In the narrow sense one may be tempted to accuse him of naïvetè, or one may take a broader view and simply say that Lissitzky was an incorrigible idealist, honest, tenacious, and—in a corrupt world— completely uncorrupted and pure. It is the measure of his humanity that he did not take the easy way out by emigrating, as did a number of his contemporaries, but decided instead to live up to his commitment and to disregard the consequences. One can only guess at the disappointment and anguish Lissitzky must have suffered after he had been cut off not only from developments in the West, but from architectural practice in Russia as well. To be great under favorable circumstances is commendable; to remain great under Stalinism is heroic. After his return to Russia Lissitzky became one of the victims of Stalin's proclamation of "Socialist realism" as the sole form of artistic expression permissible in Russia. Unwilling to join the party hacks, Lissitzky restricted himself to graphic work and exhibition architecture. One of his last creative efforts was a poster showing Hitler contemplating the shadow outline of Napoleon, with the warning written above: "Hitler, here is thy grave."

One may ask how Lissitzky, the Jew, the cosmopolitan, the Russian, and the architect, fits into the mainstream of Russian cultural history. Let us take a brief look at Russian architecture prior to the October Revolution. While conquest and territorial change in the West were usually accompanied by cultural cross-fertilization and eventual synthesis, the vast territorial extent of Russia and the special character of her relations to both East and West were responsible for a different kind of development. The most incisive events in Russian history were the Tartar and Mongol invasions, which left a three-hundred-year cultural, social, and political gap in the evolution of that country. Until the first Tartar intrusion in 1238, Russia's evolution matched developments in the rest of Europe and the East. Once Russia had accepted Christianity from Byzantium, its art and architecture drew both inspiration and strength from Christian Orthodox sources in the East, modifying and transforming these elements with the help of native traditions. These traditions had deep roots in wooden domestic architecture, which, over the centuries, had evolved into a sophisticated and extensive art. Carving, and the Russian love for decoration, go back to this tradition. The use of color also had its roots in old folk art. This, combined with Byzantine richness had given Russian architecture its peculiar national flavor, and represented one of the many sources that were absorbed into "Socialist realism," albeit in a crude and garish sort of way. According to early Russian chroniclers, Vladimir's choice of Greek Orthodoxy as the official religion (A.D. 988) "may indeed have been in part determined by aesthetic considerations."[3] The centers of early Byzantine-native architecture were Kiev, Vladimir-Suzdal, and later Novgorod and Moscow. Without going into the details of this development it may be said that this was the first and most important cultural import that had to be absorbed and transformed by the Russians. It also became the prime source of a later schism in Peter I's time. Thus, an offshoot of Byzantine culture was grafted onto the Russian tree, bearing wondrous fruit.

After 1299, Moscow became the center of the Russian Orthodox Church and the focus of all national cultural activity. Without elaborating on all the subtle changes that took place in the adaptation of Byzantine forms to Russian ecclesiastical architecture, we must note another event of considerable importance, namely, the importation of Italian architects to Moscow by Ivan III (1462–1505) and their subsequent influence on Russian architecture. This, and the victory of Dmitri Donskoi over the Mongols in 1380, made Moscow the sole national and cultural center of a unified Russia, and in turn released a veritable flood of creative energies that had previously been fragmented and sapped by disunity and the Mongol occupation. Still, the damage done by the Tartar and Mongol invasions proved permanent and has continued to affect all aspects of Russian life ever since. The saying, "Scratch a Russian and you will discover a Tartar!" is more than a joke, and Westerners would do well to keep this fact in mind when passing superficial judgments on Russia's "backwardness."

Soviet propaganda notwithstanding, and as a result of xenophobic insecurity generated by intrusions from both East and West throughout her history, Russia has developed a historical appetite for territorial expansion—the occupation of Czechoslovakia in August of 1968 being only the latest example. This drive, coupled with a desire to

---

[3] Tamara Talbot Rice, *A Concise History of Russian Art* (New York, Washington: Frederick A. Praeger, 1963), p. 8.

17

find an outlet to the Baltic, led to the foundation of St. Petersburg by Peter I in 1703. Petersburg (now Leningrad) is more than just another Russian city. It is both the symbol and the material realization of Russia's second great cultural and political transformation. Petersburg became Peter I's "window to the West," and superseded Moscow, the Byzantine-oriental capital of Russia, as the Western European capital with all that this implied for the political and cultural life of Russia. Earlier Vladimir had decided to look both East and West for the right religion to civilize and christianize his subjects; now Peter went to Holland and England to westernize and modernize the nation. This was done brutally, unequivocally, and—on the level of the ruling classes—thoroughly. Italian, French, Dutch, German, and other European artists and architects, brought to Russia by the score, transformed official art and architecture in the image of Western European styles and taste. Architecture became classical and academic, the arts borrowed from Western Europe, and the Russians had to begin the whole process of absorption and transformation anew.

A look at the structure of the two principal cities, Moscow and St. Petersburg, reveals the difference between these two worlds. Moscow—ancient, Slavic, with its Kremlin and its ring of walled monasteries at the periphery, the rest consisting of private homesteads, complete with vegetable gardens, service structures, and domestic animals— had the appearance of an overgrown village, where streets had to go around the private lots, with no municipal restrictions, and often led nowhere. St. Petersburg—preplanned, classical, with aligned streets, stone palaces, clearly zoned districts, and the Winter Palace dominating the space at the intersection of its three main radials—is essentially a Western aristocratic city, the center of a vast governmental bureaucracy, its principal streets connecting the various regimental quarters to the palace to facilitate quick military action.

The changes that carried Russia from paganism to Christianity, from political fragmentation to the establishment of a centralized, autocratic national state, did nothing to bridge the deep chasm separat ing the ruling classes from the vast population of serfs. Nor did the legal emancipation of the serfs in 1861 close the gap, for it failed to alter the material condition of the serfs in any significant way. Until the Revolution of 1917 the serfs lived and suffered in a nether world of their own. The political and psychological aftereffects of this profound and long-enduring split in Russian society cannot be overestimated.

When one adds to this the recurrent famines, political insurrections, World War I, the October Revolution, subsequent Western intervention, and World War II, one begins to glimpse the complexity of the forces that influenced the development of the USSR of today.

These historical events and their pervasive effect on every aspect of Russian life must be kept in mind if one is to understand post-Revolutionary developments in Russian architecture, and especially the present struggle to shake off the effects of the so-called "Socialist realism." Until the October Revolution, Russian architectural production remained essentially aristocratic and academic. True, some native and indigenous elements were being absorbed, but essentially inspiration was supplied by classicism and allied developments in Europe. Since the reader will find references to these developments in the text, only the most sketchy genealogy of the architectural trends that culminated in the emergence of Socialist realism will be attempted here.

Traditionally, Russian architects were totally captive to the aristocracy, their major, indeed their only, clients. While this may have been true in Europe up to the beginning of the eighteenth century, in Russia this condition prevailed virtually until the Revolution. The introduction of foreign architects—particularly after the founding of St. Petersburg—and the foundation of the St. Petersburg Academy of Arts, tied official Russian architecture firmly to classicism and eclecticism. Apart from the resulting schism between Muscovite and Petrine architecture, aristocratic taste and royal megalomania removed architecture even further from the life of the people. Interestingly enough, the Soviets later managed to accomplish an ideological somersault and to acclaim precisely this kind of architecture as closest to the ideals of Marxism and popular taste and thus, by extension, proletarian in its very essence.

With the exception of a number of limited efforts during the first half of the nineteenth century to arouse interest in Muscovite forms, classicism reigned supreme. These efforts centered around Count Anatoly Nikolaevich Demidov's attempt to launch a Slavic Revival by publishing a detailed illustrated history of Russian architecture. This movement roughly paralleled the efforts of the arts and crafts movements in the West. The emancipation of the serfs in 1861 produced a much stronger impetus toward a more thorough appreciation of medieval Russian architecture. Nationalism and reaction against Western influences led to the emergence of Russian Populism in the second half of the nineteenth century. The Populists took Russian *reality* as a point of departure for all cultural production, coupling this concept with a desire for social improvement for the broad masses. Perhaps it is here that one may recognize one of the deeper sources of Lissitzky's lifelong preoccupation with architecture as a social art. The movement inspired a new style, called "Ropetskaia" architecture (after I. P. Ropet).

Another group, similar to the Ropetskaia group, formed the so-called "Wanderers" (Peredvizhniki) movement. Centered in Abramtseva, near Moscow, this movement was financed by the railway magnate Savva Mamontov—the first time a wealthy merchant rather than an aristocrat acted as a patron of the arts in Russia. The Peredvizhniki wandered around the country and lectured the people on culture, at the same time seeking inspiration for their own creations in folk art. They believed that art should perform a double function, using the masses as its primary source of inspiration on the one hand, and acting as an agent for social change on the other. While Peter I had tried to purge Russian life of old peasant habits, the Wanderers preached the opposite, placing the humble Russian muzhik at the center of all national life. This attitude—among others—found its partial metamorphosis in Socialist realism, strange as this may seem. At the core of this attitude was the desire to evolve along strictly national lines and to ignore developments in the West.

Moving in much the same general direction as the Slavic Revivalists were the Pan-Slavists, who in addition to reviving Russian Byzantine styles, tried to reach as far as Kievan Russia for inspiration.

In the second half of the nineteenth century the first professional associations came into being: The Moscow Architectural Society was founded in 1867, and the Petersburg Architectural Society in 1871. However, these were mostly debating societies and had little impact on actual architectural production.

The first group to break away from classicism and populism was the Mir Isskustva (World of Art) Association of Architects. It grew out of a student organization, The Nevski Pickwickians, founded in the 1880's. In its aims, it was very similar to the Art Nouveau movement in the West. The Mir Isskustva group was internationally oriented and believed that art should evolve organically, unimpeded by restrictions imposed by religion, politics, society, or style, that it should spring from the soil of pure creative force. A magazine, *Mir Isskustva*, published in 1898 by this group, introduced to Russia illustrations of West European Art Nouveau. The Russian counterpart of this style was the so-called Style Moderne, but like its Western counterpart, the movement did not last very long, being more of a fad than a true style.

In the first two decades of the twentieth century there were some further attempts to revive national forms, such as a plan to restore the old cottage industries, but essentially the field belonged to the classical revivalists with deep roots in Petersburg. Even though classicism and eclecticism did not manage to penetrate all of architectural production in Russia, they nevertheless prepared the way for later developments, culminating in Stalin's decision to accept classicism and eclecticism as the *only* form of architectural expression for all of Russia.

World War I disrupted all building activity in Russia and further widened the chasm between Russian and West European developments in the arts and architecture. This aspect is well documented in the text and will not be elaborated upon here. However, the text does not mention the various post-World War I societies and associations whose philosophies played an important role in the evolution of Soviet architectural thought, and we now turn to these.

Lissitzky does refer to one of the important figures of this period, Commissar Lunacharski, who was appointed head of the Department of Fine Arts (IZO) of the Commissariat of the People's Education (NARKOMPROS), founded in 1918. Lunacharski had spent several years in exile prior to the Revolution, and during that period had met a number of avant-garde Russian artists living in Western Europe. After the Revolution these artists became his protégés and enthusiastic allies in the reconstruction of Russia's cultural life.

In 1918 the old Petersburg Academy of Arts was reformed under the auspices of IZO and renamed the Petrograd Free Studios (SVOMAS). Anyone over sixteen years of age was admitted without prerequisites. There was no rigid educational structure, professors were elected by the students, and students were allowed to join all study groups freely. The Studio as such was abolished in 1921 and later revived in a somewhat changed form as the Academy of Artistic Studies.

Developments in Moscow followed a similar course. The Higher Technical Artistic Studios (VKHUTEMAS) were established in 1918 (see Lissitzky text). Departments were independent, and rather than following a rigid professional division, consisted of a loose grouping of free workshops around professional subjects. Discussions on art were open to the public and were free of academic discipline. The Institute of Artistic Culture (INHUK) was founded soon after as a branch of IZO. It occupied itself with the investigation of theoretical issues concerning art under Communism. Its initial program was written by Wassily Kandinsky, but was turned down by a majority vote. Kandinsky left INHUK, and later went to Germany to take part in the work of the Bauhaus movement.

Although founded as early as 1906, an organization called PROLE-CULT became important only after the Revolution. It adopted a program that was somewhat reminiscent of the Wanderers movement. Its concern was the implementation of the Communist program by the widest mobilization of the workers and the masses for cultural work. The various branches of the trade unions were to be the vehicle for this mobilization. Many of the artists who belonged to INHUK were also members of PROLECULT. The theories espoused by these artists, i.e., constructivism, objectivism, suprematism, and futurism, are explained in the text.

Until the proclamation in 1921 of Lenin's New Economic Policy (NEP), which reintroduced elements of capitalism in both manufacturing and agriculture, these avant-garde artists had a virtual monopoly on all artistic production in the Soviet Union. The emergence of a relatively independent economic element broke this uncontested suzerainty of the PROLECULT, thereby allowing conservative voices to be heard once again. The degree to which these developments have influenced subsequent events is difficult to assess.

Thus, in the early stages of the Revolution, developments in the arts and architecture were in the hands of the avant-garde and the cultural radical left. At that time it was convenient for the Communist party to allow the development of various trends and to let the artists vie for the favor of official approval. The triumph of Bolshevism over its internal and external enemies and the creation of a monolithic bureaucratic state structure, together with the introduction of the first Five-Year Plan (see text) changed this situation; henceforth cultural efforts were forced into the same conformist mold as all other facets of Soviet life. A monolithic, bureaucratic, one-party system precluded tolerance of diverse views in the area of culture and the arts. All views had to conform to a single interpretation of art as part of a general party line imposed from the top. The ultimate outcome of all this is well documented and described in Part III of the Appendix.

The official date of the demise of modern architecture in Russia is April 23, 1932, when the Communist party of the USSR issued a decree "Concerning the Reorganization of Literary-artistic Societies" and established the monolithic Union of Artists. This became the parent organization for all other artistic associations, including the Union of Soviet Architects (SSA), which in turn replaced all other existing architectural associations and promptly imposed its own interpretation of architectural expression, (i.e., Socialist realism = classical eclecticism) on all aspects of Soviet architecture.

Lissitzky's work must be seen in this context. To decry the *reality* of the situation seems futile and hypocritical, for the *potential* of his ideas represents the essence of Lissitzky's contribution. His ideas were decades ahead of the *Zeitgeist* of the first half of the twentieth century. Not unlike one of his Prouns, Lissitzky seems suspended between East and West—partaking in the social revolution of one and the artistic revolution of the other—he is more than a name, or an influence, or a solitary genius. He is the symbol of a bridge which will have to be built between Russia and the West, a bridge that will allow a free flow of ideas in both directions, unimpeded by the roadblocks of history, ideology, and fear.

Lissitzky, the Russian, the Jew, the Communist who dared return to a hostile homeland, the internationalist who knew Berlin and Paris, but who also knew Vitebsk and Moscow, is more than just another "pioneer of modern architecture," for he returned and chanced oblivion, suffered, and kept the faith—never retreating one single step from his position and his belief that the task of architecture in the twentieth century was primarily a social one. For he knew that the seed he had planted would grow.

True, Soviet Socialist realism was a defeat for the new architecture, but is it not equally true that modern architectural eclecticism has arrived at a parallel stylistic impasse in the West?

Judging by the Russian underground literary production that is currently startling the West with its brilliance and depth, it is only a matter of time before the other arts will follow suit. Even now Soviet architecture is beginning to free itself from the shackles of classicism, and functional buildings are replacing the ornate "wedding cakes" of the preceding decades. One reason for this change is that the rational application of modern industrialized building techniques has been successfully achieved in the USSR. Such a development effectively discourages the urge to apply classical ornamentation or similar uneconomical follies. Given a better political climate and a reallocation of resources, Russia's architectural situation should improve radically and thoroughly in the near future.

This translation of Lissitzky's writings, the publication of Sophie Lissitzky's monograph, and the growing interest in Lissitzky's work both here in the West and in Russia certainly indicate that something is happening in the collective subconscious of the architects on both sides of the Iron Curtain. Among his numerous and equally brilliant contemporaries in the field of architecture, El Lissitzky emerges as the only one whose commitment to the social purpose of architecture was endorsed with his own life. This, combined with a most profound sense of humanity, seems to be the key to his character and the primary source of his appeal. No evaluation of his work can ignore this commitment, or fail to take into account the moral strength that enabled him to persist in it in the face of the impossible situation he encountered on his courageous return to Russia.

On the occasion of his death, his wife wrote, "An *honorable* Communist has left us. Right to the end he pledged all his powers to the *just* cause of his people. He demanded the impossible of himself, yet in his continual dedication he enriched his life. 'For I am a human being, and that means being a fighter.' These words of Goethe were endorsed by El Lissitzky with his life."[4]

---

[4] Lissitzky-Küppers, *op. cit.*, p. 102.

Russia: An Architecture for World Revolution

Basic Premises

The birth of the machine signaled the onset of the technological revolution, which destroyed the handicrafts and played an essential role in the rise of large-scale modern manufacture. In the course of a single century new production systems transformed all aspects of life. Modern technology not only revolutionized social and economic developments but aesthetic ones as well. The basic elements of new architecture in Western Europe and America were determined by this revolution.

October 1917 marked the beginning of the Russian Revolution and the opening of a new page in the history of human society. It is to this social revolution, rather than to the technological revolution, that the basic elements of Russian architecture are tied.

The individual, private client has now been replaced by the so-called "social commission." Emphasis has shifted from the intimate and the individual to the public and the universal. Today, architecture must be judged according to different criteria. The whole field of architecture has now become a problem. And what is more, in Russia this problem had to be faced by a country exhausted by war and hunger and tightly sealed off from the rest of the world. These new architectural problems could not be solved until a foundation had been provided by the restoration of order in the economy. Prewar production levels were quickly achieved. For our present needs, however, such prewar levels and rates of production are inadequate. To be effective and to fulfill our mission in the world, we must strive to accelerate the rate of growth, to force the pace. This can only be accomplished if we do not limit ourselves to what we have inherited but, instead, completely reconstruct it. We must not only build, but rebuild. We are rebuilding industry, we are rebuilding agriculture. This restructuring of production creates a new conception of life that nurtures culture, including, of course, architecture. Our new architecture does not just attempt to complete something that has been temporarily interrupted. On the contrary, it is poised on the threshold of the future and committed to more than mere construction. Its task is to comprehend the new conditions of life, so that by the creation of responsive building design it can actively participate in the full realization of the new world. Thus the thrust of Soviet architecture is directed toward the goal of reconstruction.

Interrelationships Between the Arts

Russian architecture, under the influence of Western Europe, succumbed—several centuries ago—to the domination of the Court, and
was relegated to the care of the Academy. There, in the company of
the other arts, architecture languished, semidormant and totally
uncreative, leading a pseudoexistence. In Russia, only individuals
licensed by the state were permitted to build, though anybody was
"free" to paint or to write poetry. Thus, the practice of architecture
merely fostered diligence, while painting fostered talent.

New artistic aspirations flourished in the fertile soil of bourgeois
Moscow, supported by the great merchants, rather than in the
aristocratic-bureaucratic atmosphere of Petersburg. Due to this support
the arts advanced at an increasingly rapid pace. Developments in
painting were pushed so radically and thoroughly that they culminated
in the investigation of the most fundamental elements of the art. Art
became more and more isolated. It found itself facing an abyss, with all
art problems tending to degenerate into questions of *l'art pour l'art* or
fashionable salon events, just as is now the case in the West. The
Revolution rechanneled this stream of energy. It suddenly offered the
radical artist such enormous scope for his activities that it will require
the work of generations to fulfill these possibilities. Simultaneously, it
introduced the concept of art as a form of cultural labor, which will in
turn have a decisive effect on the reconstruction of our architecture.

The changing interrelationship between the newly emerging arts is
another important factor that vitally affects the basic elements of
modern architecture. The influence of the arts on architecture has been
valuable and extraordinary, but has also brought some dangers in its
wake. Our art belongs to the age of science. We employ the methods
of our age—we analyze. Experimentation in painting is the least
hampered by the medium. Thus, the new creative forces in art have
uncovered the basic elements of three-dimensional design by a process
of analysis. In the course of this work two distinct and clearly defined
views have emerged:

"The world is given us through vision, through color" epitomizes
one of these views. "The world is given to us through touch, through
materials" represents the other. Both comprehend the world in terms
of geometric order. The first conception calls for pure spectral colors,

abstractly included in the rational order of geometric elements, i.e., a color planimetry, a world of crystalline structure. This world is built up in visual, infinite space. Brought to its logical conclusion, such thinking eventually led to the complete renunciation of the color spectrum, with the result that everything was reduced to a planimetric figure scheme (black and white). Painting as such ceased to exist and turned to the design of purely abstract volumetric forms. The architectural character of these stereometric forms was immediately recognized. Thus, painting became a transfer point for architecture. A new asymetrical equilibrium of volumes was constructed, the tensions between the solids were given new dynamic expression, and a new rhythmic order was developed. Since the leading exponent of the color theory was a painter (Malevich), he failed to recognize the objective reality of the world. Because he always looked at it only through his own eyes, he remained trapped in a world devoid of real objects. The broader implications of this had to be developed by us, the architects.

The second conception of the world via the medium of matter required both a visual and a tactile perception of things. In this case the whole design process tends to emanate from the specific characteristics of the respective medium used. The leader of this movement (Tatlin) assumed—quite independently of the rational and scientific methods of technology—that the intuitive and artistic mastery of materials would lead to inventions on the basis of which objects could be constructed. He believed that he could prove this theory with his design for the *"Monument to the Third International"* (1920). He accomplished this task without having any special technical knowledge of construction, thus proving his assumption. This represents one of the first attempts to achieve a synthesis between the technical and the artistic. The efforts of the new architecture to loosen up volumes and to create a spatial interpenetration between outside and inside found their early expression in this work. Here, an ancient concept of form, as represented for example by the Sargon Pyramid at Khorsabad, was actually recreated in a new material for a new content. This effort, as well as a later series of experiments with materials and models, gave birth to the term "constructivism." The present "constructivist" generation of professional architects looks upon this work as formalistic or even "symbolic." Later we shall return to this subject and take issue with this type of dialectic. One thing can be established right now: these accomplishments in the sister arts have contributed significantly to the reconstruction of our architecture.

Plates 3, 4

At first these pioneers were not able to build. The war had interrupted all construction acitivities. During the early revolutionary years old building materials were carried away to be used as fuel for heating purposes. This created vacant sites. New construction personnel had to be trained. The function of educating young architects was retained by the schools, which had to develop new methods. Paralleling the above-mentioned developments in painting was the formation of a synthetic movement led by architects (Architecture + Painting + Sculpture). These young architects, themselves still trained in classical schools, had to shed their own skin first. Their first act had to be one of destruction, of rupture with the past. Theirs was a struggle for expression.

The task was clear—it consisted in elevating architecture in terms of its artistic and pragmatic values to a level consistent with the values of our own age. These ideas assured the victory of youth in the schools. Youth was involved in the total content of life, while the old academicians had nothing to offer in return but borrowed, foreign, and long-corrupt theories.

Youth set itself the goal of achieving the synthesis between utilitarian tasks and architectural concepts of space. At first, in the early stages of development, actual conditions failed to provide the opportunity for real projects. Thus, projects had to be invented for imaginary sites **Fig. 1** (for instance, a restaurant and landing place on a cliff).

Whereas usually an organic realization achieves full form by a process of selection, in this instance much was accomplished in the realm of pure design ideas. This carried with it the danger of reverting to extreme solutions. The elaboration of new methods for the scientific-objective elucidation of the elements of architectural design—such as mass, surface, space, proportion, rhythm, etc.—was decisive in establishing the distinctive character of the new schools. A new methodology had to be created. This work, begun by such pioneers as Ladovski, Dokuchaiev, and Krinski, was continued by men of the younger generation, such as Balikhin, Korshev, Lamtsov, and others. Contemporary schools must not only train builders and designers but must also educate architects who work in their own field as scientists.

This serious work on the basic elements of architecture called for the mobilization of all the vital energies available. A group was formed which placed the main emphasis on construction and which demanded the direct application of the methods of the engineer and the builder to architecture. Form was to result directly from construction. Inter-

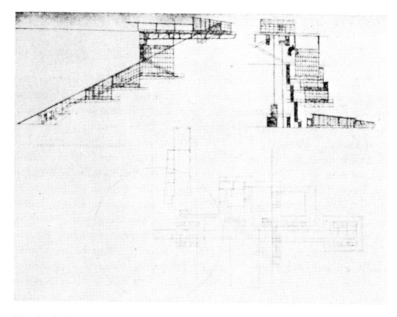

Fig. 1. Atelier Ladovski (Vkhutein 1923): Restaurant and landing platform
on a cliff.

national architecture displays this tendency, but in the content of our
situation there is a basic difference that must be taken into account. In
all countries except Russia technical achievements can be counted on
as a given quantity of modern life. In America the architect has a direct
and continuing relationship with technology. Perhaps this is why he
does not ask more from technology than it can offer. In our country
it is still impossible to have such urban complexes as are found in Paris,
Chicago, or Berlin. It is through technology that we can build a bridge
to all the most recent achievements, which is what made it possible for
our country to pass directly from the hoe to the tractor without having
to travel the long path of historical development. That is why we want
to introduce the most modern methods of building and construction
into our country—and why we see the works and designs of both the
"formalists" and the "constructivists" as a radical experiment in the
manipulation of construction.

First Projects

In 1923, Soviet architecture was presented with its first new task. A plan was advanced to build a massive complex in the center of Moscow, a so-called "Palace of Labor", for the new collective ruler, the worker. It was to serve for large congresses, mass rallies, meetings, theatrical productions, and so on. The task was as colossal as were the times. However, time had yet to produce a crystallization of definite architectural concepts. Thus, most of the proposed designs were amorphous and fragmented conglomerations, drawing their inspiration both from the past and from the mechanistic present, and based to a large degree on literary rather than architectural ideas. The design of the three brothers Vesnin marks the first step away from destruction toward new construction. By elevating a closed plan by means of an exposed **Fig. 2** reinforced concrete frame, a clear stereometric volume is produced. **Plate 12** The whole is still conceived as an isolated, single object, independent of urban design considerations. The compulsion to rely on columnar organization remains pervasive. The complex is crowned by a romantic allusion to radio-tower technology, and the large space designed to accommodate 8,000 persons is still completely conventional. Nevertheless, this design represents the first attempt to create a new form for a social task that in itself was still ill-defined at the time. The ensuing period offered an increasing number of more concrete tasks, their purpose and aim becoming gradually more defined, and what was accomplished improved accordingly.

In 1924, the brothers A. A. and V. A. Vesnin worked out a design for the office building of the newspaper *Leningradskaia Pravda*. The building lot measured a mere 6 × 6 meters. The design of this building represents a characteristic solution in a period yearning for glass, steel, and concrete. All accessories—which on a typical city street are usually **Fig. 3** tacked onto the building—such as signs, advertising, clocks, loudspeakers, **Plate 11** and even the elevators inside, have been incorporated as integral elements of the design and combined into a unified whole. This is the aesthetic of constructivism.

The first small building that gave clear evidence of the reconstruction of our architecture was the Soviet Pavilion at the Paris World's Fair **Fig. 4** of 1925, designed by Melnikov. The close proximity of the Soviet **Plates 1?** Pavilion to other creations of international architecture revealed in the **14**

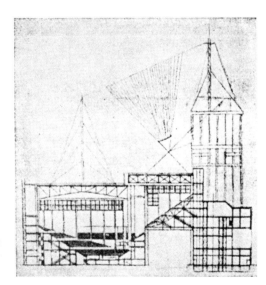

Fig. 2. Brothers Vesnin:
Palace of Labor, 1923.
Top: Section.
Bottom: Plan.

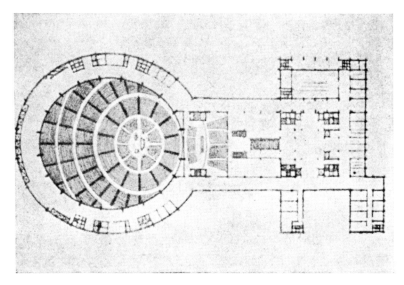

most glaring way the fundamentally different attitudes and concepts
embodied in Soviet architecture. This work represents the "formalistic"
wing of the radical front of our architecture, a group whose primary
aim was to work out a fitting architectural concept for each utilitarian task.

33

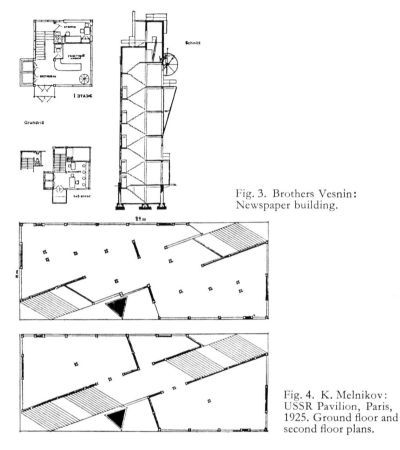

Fig. 3. Brothers Vesnin: Newspaper building.

Fig. 4. K. Melnikov: USSR Pavilion, Paris, 1925. Ground floor and second floor plans.

In this case, the basic concept represents an attempt to loosen up the over-all volume by exposing the staircase. In the plan, the axis of symmetry is established on the diagonal, and all other elements are rotated by 180°. Hence, the whole has been transposed from ordinary symmetry at rest into symmetry in motion. The tower element has been transformed into an open system of pylons. The structure is built honestly of wood, but instead of relying on traditional Russian log construction employs modern wood construction methods. The whole is transparent. Unbroken colors. Therefore no false monumentality. A new spirit.

Housing Communes

Housing is one of the most pressing problems in all of Europe. In the West it was simply a matter of resuming construction activities where they had left off before the war, though under changed economic and technical conditions. In Russia, however, this became a question of solving a new social problem of fundamental cultural significance. In our country all existing differences in housing accommodation, from a hole in a basement for the worker in a large city, a multiroom high-rise apartment to a private villa, have been abrogated. The Soviet architect was given the task of establishing a new standard of housing by devising a new type of housing unit, not intended for single individuals in conflict with each other as in the West, but for the masses. A good existing example of this type of housing is the log cabin, still used by the great masses of the rural population, which over the centuries has developed appropriate structural and technical construction standards. Even though these houses are the product of the handicrafts, they are in all other respects, as for instance in the development of individual parts, a standardized mass-production effort with each part developed and fixed in such a way that the builder can easily assemble the parts by himself (dry assembly). The same system was also used in the cities until industrialization produced the split between city and country.

The dwellings in the city of Moscow are built of wood . . . the roofs are covered with wood shingles . . . hence, the great conflagrations. Those whose houses have burned down can procure new ones: Outside the city walls one can find on display in a special market a number of houses ready for assembly. They are available at reasonable cost and can be easily assembled on any other building site. The above-described house market is located in a certain district of the city . . ., the purchased house can be delivered within two days ready for assembly in any other disctrict of the city. The timber framework has been precut and matched and it remains only to fill the crevices with moss . . .   A. Olearius (1636), *Journey to Moscavium*

I quote this excerpt in order to document the healthy collective impulses that have always existed within the people and also to prove that uniformity and standardization did not result in superficiality.

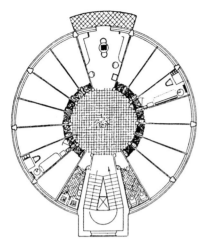

Fig. 5. Kotsar (Vkhutein): Bachelor apartments. Plan.

In the future it will be necessary on the one hand to establish a balance between the intimate and individualistic demands for housing, and on the other to take full account of general social conditions. Thus, for example, cooking should be transferred from the private single kitchen into the communal cooking laboratory; the main meal should be consumed in public eating establishments; and the rearing of children should become the responsibility of the kindergarten or the school. In this way all the spaces essential to the individual's intimate life can be defined and isolated from the sum total of the over-all housing shortage in terms of both present and future needs. Conversely, communal facilities should become ever more flexible in size and design. By taking such a stance, architecture becomes the expression of a social condition and attains new validity by becoming an effective element in the life of society. Presently our goal is the transition from housing as an agglomeration of many private dwellings to housing communes.

The construction activities of the communal administration and the large central cooperatives have resulted in a one-sided attack on the housing shortage in our country, because until recently these efforts have not led to any radical experiments in the field of new housing. The architectural faculty of Vkhutemas was asked by the Building

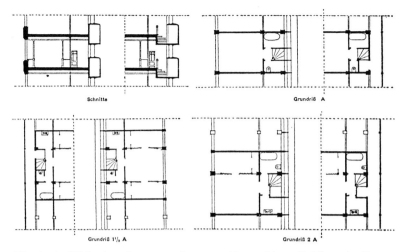

Schnitte   Grundriß A

Grundriß 1½ A   Grundriß 2 A

Fig. 6. A. Zilchenko: Apartment layouts with corridors dividing the floors.

Department of the Mossoviet to work on a project that called for the planning and design implementation of a human settlement. One of their solutions is presented here to serve as an example: a circular tower, consisting of individual dwelling units 6 × 9 meters in size and planned as a home for single persons. All general activities are designed to take place in an adjacent communal structure.

Economy is one of the governing factors in this proposal. The grouping together of a large number of housing units produces arcade-like corridors and results in the reduction of the over-all number of stairwells.

Zilchenko's split-level corridor is an interesting invention. He places the main corridor near the exterior wall, thus providing the rooms behind the corridor with direct daylight, while at the same time reducing the number of necessary stairwells. The apartments are located along the corridor and consist of one-, one-and-a-half-, and two-room units, each having its own bathroom and kitchen facilities. Obviously, such a system could be applied to a number of other structures as well. Genuinely new building types can be evolved in this manner. Such new systems stimulate the economy to produce new materials, provide the designer with concrete and reliable form elements, and suggest to the cultural pioneer new possibilities for community formation. One of the governmental agencies doing such radical work was the Building

37

Committee of the Economic Council of the R.S.F.S.R. Here, housing problems were systematically researched, which lead to a number of proposals by architects Ginsburg, Pasternak, Vladimirov and Barshit. So far, the following types have been developed:

Type A : Blocks of ordinary individual apartments have been transformed into a housing commune by the introduction of a full-length **Fig. 7** corridor lined with single rooms in the lower stories. This corridor

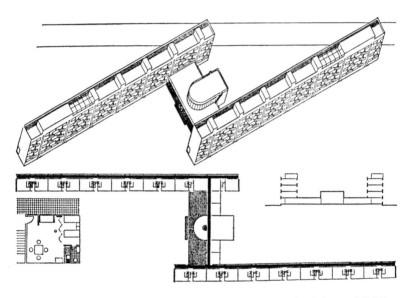

Fig. 7. Building Committee of the Economic Council of the R.S.F.S.R.: Housing commune, type A.

provides a connection between the stairwells and the communal center (dining room, rest room, children's playroom, and so on).

Type E : A housing commune consisting of 360 individual rooms, **Fig. 8** each designed for a single person only. There are six levels divided into two equal parts, three stories each. Horizontal traffic is carried by two corridors on the second and fifth levels. Small, open staircases connect the corridors with landings on floors below and above. Each landing serves four of the single rooms. The staircases are placed parallel to the long axis of the building, forming a unified system from the bottom

38

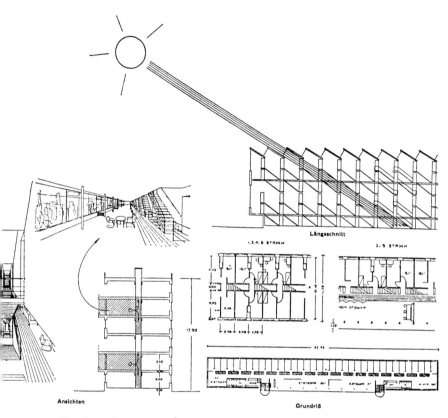

Fig. 8. Building Committee of the Economic Council of the R.S.F.S.R.: Housing commune, type E.

to the top, and receive direct daylight by means of a glazed shed roof. The corridors are central and have been widened near the communal rooms.

Fig. 9   *Type F* is characterized by a corridor serving two stories. The dwelling units are one-and-a-half stories high with a 3.25–3.50 meters high living room and a 2.15–2.25 meters high sleeping nook with adjacent bathroom. The space saved by lowering the sleeping nooks has been used for the corridor. This corridor connects the dwelling block with the community center, with its complex of kitchens, dining rooms, reading halls, recreation rooms, and children's playrooms.

39

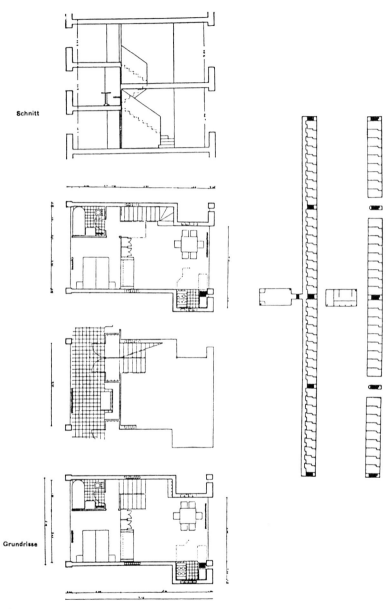

Schnitt

Grundrisse

Fig. 9. Building Committee of the Economic Council of the R.S.F.S.R.:
Housing commune, type F.

40

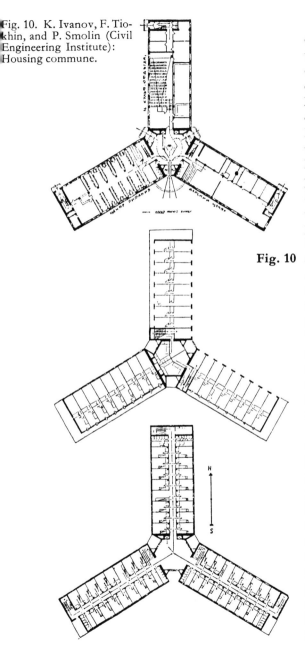

Fig. 10. K. Ivanov, F. Tiokhin, and P. Smolin (Civil Engineering Institute): Housing commune.

Fig. 10

All these systems are quite flexible and lend themselves to a number of variations, depending on the type of building lot, the desired number of housing units, etc. Let us look at another type of solution for a housing commune, proposed by the Leningrad Building Institute. The design consists of a compact, centralized, tri-axial building volume of six stories for 660 tenants. A single corridor serves three floors. The dwelling units consist of two and three rooms, respectively. Three basic types of community rooms (dining, children's care, and recreation) are located on the first floor in a separate wing of each complex.

It is not important whether the scheme favors a horizontal (corridor) or a vertical (staircase) system; the important thing is that the housing block, which up to now has merely represented the algebraic sum of self-contained private apartments, has now been transformed into a synthetic complex for total communal

41

living. Once the functions of the individual elements become better defined, it will be much easier to design the over-all structure in a more flexible way. At the same time it will be possible to give more consideration to individual desires.

All these inventions and the restructuring of individual elements have one goal in common: to determine the direction in which the housing of a Socialistic society should develop. This then, represents one of the central tasks in the reconstruction of our architecture.

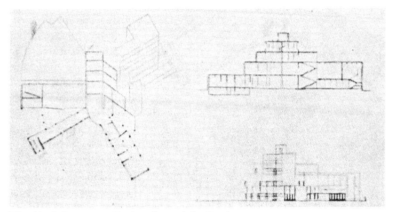

Fig. 11. I. Lamtsov: Design for a club. Sections.

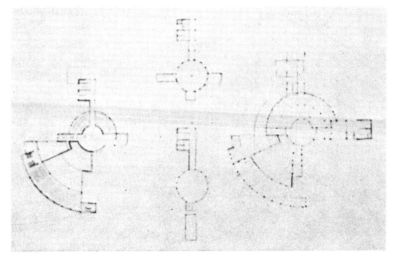

Fig. 12. I. Lamtsov: Design for a club. Plans.

The Club as a Social Force

Buildings designed to serve all of society have always acted as a repository of the sum total of all creative energies. Depending on the prevalent social order, these have usually been of either a religious or a governmental character: the Church and the Palace. These were the power sources of the old order. Their power can only be transcended by establishing new power sources belonging to our new order. Some years ago it was thought that palaces would serve this purpose, except that now they were to be called "Palaces of Labor." This created the danger of introducing a foreign and superficial pathos into our lives. If the term "palace" is to be applied to our situation at all, and in order for it to have any validity in our situation, it is the factories that should be transformed into "Palaces of Labor" first. The competition of 1923 for the "Palace of Labor" in Moscow represented a new departure in this direction and marks the beginning of a great number of competitions for similar palaces, later called "Palaces of Culture," which in turn eventually came to be known quite simply as "Clubs."

In the course of this work three phases of development can be traced:

1. The remodeling of existing buildings that had previously served different functions, and their subsequent transformation into clubs.
2. The building of new complexes. However, it was soon discovered that the conglomeration of diverse and unrelated individual elements, consisting of the theater hall (old baroque system) and the motion-picture hall, both surrounded by corridors and individual rooms, did not offer a good solution for the new cultural task.
3. Only gradually were attempts made to resolve this task by a complete restructuring of the problem.

The growing needs in this area helped to bring about a clearer understanding of the whole problem. To achieve a solution, new spatial volumes and construction methods had to be created capable of providing all the age groups of the working masses with facilities for recreation and relaxation after a day's work, i.e., a place to store up new sources of energy. Here each child, each adolescent, each adult, as well as all the older people, could be educated into becoming collective human beings outside the circle of their families, while their individual interests could be enlarged and broadened at the same time. The aim of the club is to liberate man and not to oppress him as was formerly done by the Church and the State.

It would be shortsighted to think that such a building could be invented in one try by a so-called architectural "genius." What we demand from the Soviet architect is that, as an artist and because of his perceptive intellect, he will fully comprehend and amplify the faintest ripple of developing energies much sooner than the masses—who tend to be shortsighted as far as their own growth is concerned—and that he will transform this energy into tangible architectural form.

We present in Fig. 13 the design for a club, planned as the center of a settlement. The club rooms and the service rooms are located along two **Fig. 13** perpendicular axes. The large theater hall and the smaller auditorium are **Plate 19** situated radially. Each successive floor recedes toward the top in a step-like manner, and the whole is grouped around a vertical axis.

A conceptual expansion of the problem yields the following propositions:

The large park grounds are to be organized in such a way that a number of open, half-open, and closed rooms will form a unified whole, responding to the functions of club life. The club ought to become a gathering place where the individual becomes one with the collective and where he stores up new reserves of energy, while he should at the same time be given the opportunity to split off and join smaller groups for the pursuit of special activities. Thus, both small and large rooms must be conceived in an organic manner, while the whole should form a new unified spatial relationship. In this context, the Roman bath, old monastery layouts, or theater plans, can no longer serve as models. It is evident that flexible rooms will have to be created to allow for different uses and variable circulation patterns. The most important thing to remember is that in the club the masses should provide for themselves, that they should not throng there from the outside merely to seek amusement, but that they should instead arrive at a realization of their potentialities by their own efforts. The club's role is to become a University of Culture. If one accepts the premise that private dwellings should strive to operate on the basis of the greatest possible austerity, then by contrast, public dwellings should provide the maximum of available luxury accessible to all. The term "reconstruction" is therefore not applicable to this case, since there is no building precedent in the past that by virtue of its social significance would provide us with a prototype

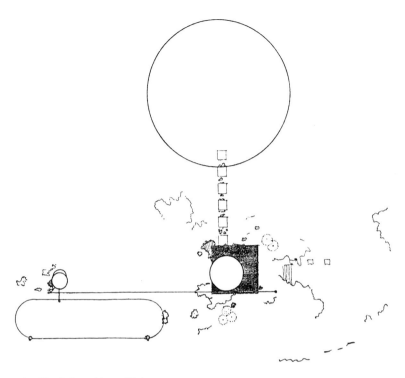

Fig. 13. I. Leonidov: Club.

solution. Here, both internal and external form must become the concrete expression of our concept of the spiritual condition and the
aesthetic life of social man.

45

Sports

The close relationship between mental and physical training suggests a similar affinity between sports structures and clubs. The new society desires a strong generation, for strength is equated with optimism and the joy of living. This explains why "physculture" enjoys equal rank with the other elements that make up the totality called "social culture." In our society so-called sports records are irrelevant. Physculture, i.e., the culture of the body, is important.

All trade unions possess their own sports grounds. The largest sports complex of this kind is being built on the outskirts of Moscow, along the most beautiful stretch of the shores of the Moskva River, the Lenin Hills rising from the right bank, the opposite shore being flat and even. Shown in plate 23 is one of the most interesting designs for this project: **Plate 23** a sports complex on the left bank of the Moskva, on a site where the river forms a large sweeping semicircle. The largest part of the complex consists of a colossal autodrome. Its outline is determined by the semi-circular shape of the site and also by the traffic pattern. A number of stadia are located within and outside the autodrome. The river bank itself has been developed into an aerodrome. The most characteristic and striking feature of the design is the structure of the grandstand. It consists of a huge, bracket-like superstructure of reinforced concrete and steel-rib construction. The autodrome is on the lowest level. Below are **Fig. 14** a number of rows of seats covered by a projecting canopy whose top **Plate 23** surface is designed to serve for bicycle and motorcycle racing. More rows of seats rise up to a break in the structure, which from that point on projects forward again. Five rows of enclosed booths are suspended from the underside of this cantilever.

The V-form of the grandstand has a double advantage: the viewing distance from the last row is only slightly greater than from the front one, and the upper seats provide a protective roof for the lower ones. Here, elements of structure and design have been consciously combined. Plans for the right bank near the Lenin Hills have been developed by the ASNOVA-Group under the leadership of Ladovski, who designed the stadia complex of the "Red Sports International."

Institutes of public hygiene are closely related to physculture. In Russia the bath has a very specific character—it is a steambath. The village has traditionally solved the problem in a very simple way: usually

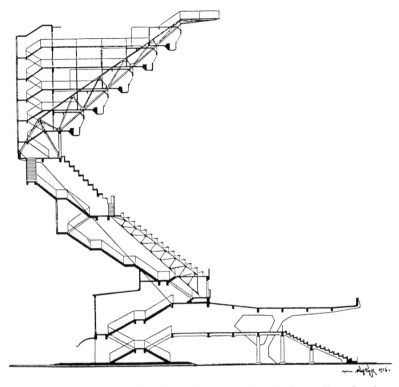

Fig. 14. M. Korshev: Section through the grandstand of a stadium for the city of Moscow, 1926.

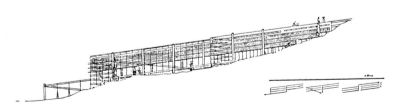

Fig. 15. Afanessiev (Vkhutein): Spa hotel.

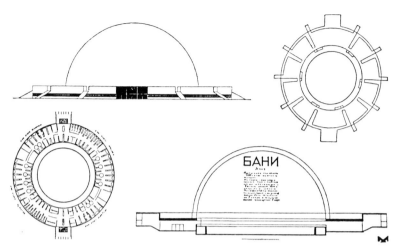

Fig. 16. Atelier A. Nikolski: Bathhouse for the city of Leningrad.

a small hut with a large stove was placed next to the village well. The city on the other hand developed the public bath house with its large communal steamroom. The floating swimming pools in the rivers used during the summer and the large bathing facilities on the Russian Riviera, which take up one third of the whole Black Sea coast from the Crimea to Batum, are used by the Russian population as open-air bathing establishments. Formerly, these facilities were accessible only to the propertied classes. Now, the whole coast has been declared a national recreational area and is being intensively developed to accommodate the vast number of vacationers crowding the beaches. In the design of these facilities two contradictory elements have to be reconciled: the free and organic growth of nature, seen as an entity of stone, vegetation, and water, as opposed to unity created by man. All this must be combined and ordered in harmony with the sensibilities and spirit of our time.

The conceptual aspect of this problem may be approached from two basically different vantage points: singular order, i.e., an order directly aimed at the whole, and organic order, or geometric order, i.e., an order based on uninhibited inner growth. The design of a facility on the shores **Fig. 15** of the Black Sea (Fig. 15) may serve as an example.

The planning of the building follows the slope of the shore with a corridor 200 meters long, flanked by the dwelling units. This represents

Plate 26 geometrical order. There is a plan afoot to build, adjacent to the massive main building, a system of easily assembled housing units that could be erected at various locations according to personal preference and as required during the bathing season—in other words, a prefabricated standard unit for individuals or families, easy to assemble. Everybody picks his own location out of the available sites. The unity of a camp site develops. Modern mechanical services are provided only on a community scale. This represents an attempt to achieve a synthesis between individual freedom and collective interdependence.

Fig. 16 One example of a solution for a citybath house is described below. The circular layout is planned as a large garden. From the outside one enters

Plate 25 directly on to the flat roof and into the sun bath. The swimming pool is located in the center. It is covered by a glass dome that can be opened during the summer months. The individual baths for both men and women are located to the right and left along the circular periphery and are sunk two meters below the ground for the sake of lower construction costs.

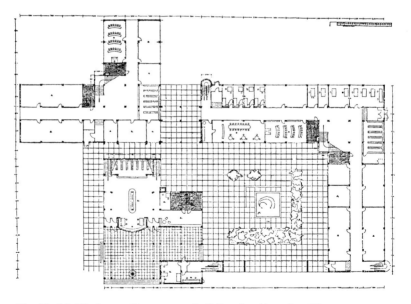

Fig. 17. M. Ginsburg: Government building for Alma-Ata. Plan.

49

Old Cities—New Buildings

A new social order is being realized in an agricultural country. We have inherited cities as different as Moscow and Samarkand, or Novosibirsk and Alma-Ata, each belonging to widely differing cultural stages. In these cities, buildings which in the past had satisfied the needs of a feudal culture are now expected to serve completely new purposes. On weekdays their streets and squares have had to adjust to an entirely new traffic rhythm and have also had to create new possibilities in terms of their function and use during holidays. Until recently, little time had been devoted to the solution of these very fundamental urban problems. The urgent need for offices for the centralized economy, for government offices of the new autonomous republics, and so on, had to be satisfied first. A number of such buildings have been constructed in Moscow

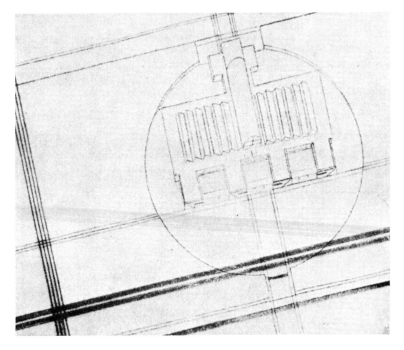

Fig. 18. Atelier A. Nikolski: School for 1000 children.

(State Trade Center), in Kharkov (Palace of Industry of the Supreme
Economic Council), and in the Siberian "Chicago," Novosibirsk. All
these were conceived as modern office structures, built in reinforced
concrete, with sharp projections and large glass surfaces. The huge
dimensions of these massive buildings are an expression of new power
rather than one of new ideas in design. They are starkly bare, their
volumes are plain and stereometric, and the traditional elements of
their monumental façades have been transformed into a series of
horizontal strips of concrete and glass. The steel construction of the
windows provides the only rhythmic articulation of the wall. In each
building one can find visual features that create new spatial effects.
Nevertheless, all this still belongs to the past. Just as in the past,
houses follow a continuous street line, as if the individual lots of
private owners still existed. There is no suggestion whatever of the new
situation in land ownership. The new houses put up so far give us no
indication of the new concept of the open street, or of the city as the

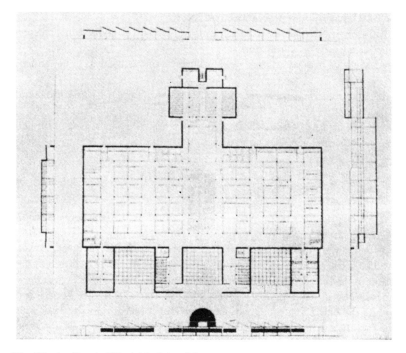

Fig. 19. Atelier A. Nikolski: School for 1000 children.

51

expression of a relationship of new associations as a result of which mass and space may be organized in a different way—even in the old parts of the city.

This new social attitude toward all problems suggests a number of new proposals. The introduction of new building types into the old fabric of the city affects the whole by transforming it.

Let us examine a design for a government building, proposed for Alma-Ata, the capital of the Kazakh Autonomous Republic. The city **Fig. 17** is located deep in Asia but was planned by Europeans. The new **Plate 30** open design of the proposed building complex will certainly affect the character and the planning of the system of all future streets and open squares in the city.

Another example is a school for 1000 children, designed in A. Nikolski's **Figs. 18,** studio. It is not a multistory building in some tight street, but a city **19** district in itself. The guidelines: new pedagogy, hygiene, economy.

1. Single-story construction permits optimum admission of daylight while providing a compact plan.
2. Classrooms (standardized) can be easily subdivided in clusters according to age group.
3. Service rooms (dining and utilities) can be used as independent units.
4. Laboratories and workshops are isolated from the classrooms and labs.
5. The center of the whole layout—an assembly hall with a sunken platform—can also be used for sports events.

Economy:
1. No stairs.
2. No scaffolding during construction.

The large offices of the State Planning Commission, the centralization of administration, and the design offices for the complete industrialization of the country call for completely new types of office structures.

The illustration (Fig. 20) of a design for the main office building of the **Fig. 20** Central Industrial Administration is a further example of these new **Plate 33** ideas. The circular plan provides a traffic link at the first-floor level, while the entire space below is left open and contains only the entrances to the offices of the individual industrial departments, located above in separate buildings. The main tower houses the administrative offices. Attached to it is the employees' club with all communal facilities. A very

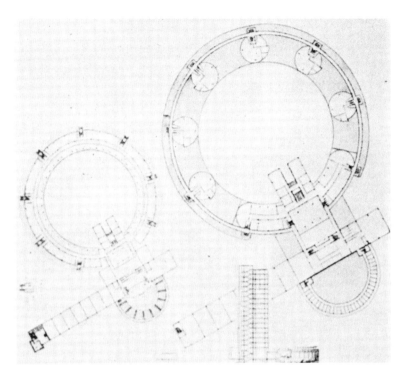

Fig. 20. A. Zilchenko (Vkhutein): Office building for the Central Industrial Administration.

direct and simple orientation system has been created by means of elementary geometrical forms.

Fig. 21   The Central Consumer Cooperatives of the USSR have sponsored a
Plate 37 competition for the design of their administration building. One of the entries is reproduced here. The design of this building is based on a new point of view. Until recently, and according to traditional ways, it was customary to string together individual buildings serving various needs in such a manner that the building line along the sidewalk was eventually completely built up, and this, in turn, produced more or less interesting façades.

In the design shown here, the closed narrow end of the building faces the street. The workrooms are located away from the street along a long wall facing a garden. The only element running parallel to the street is

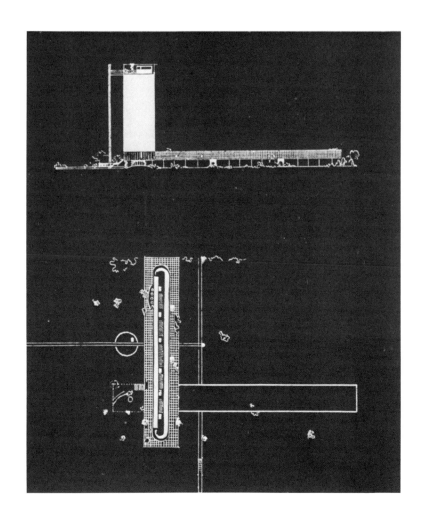

Fig. 21. I. Leonidov: Office Building for the Union of Cooperatives.

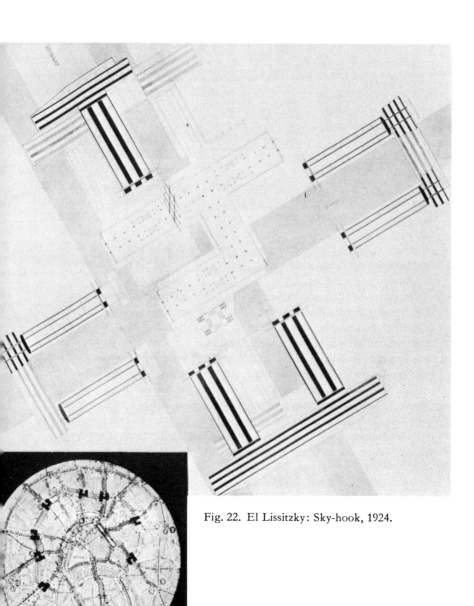

Fig. 22. El Lissitzky: Sky-hook, 1924.

Fig. 23. Moscow: City center with sky-hooks around the inner ring road.

55

a low exhibition building. The design of the large building places the entrances below, with a hall above taking care of traffic distribution and the cloakrooms. Then come the office floors, and at the top the club-rooms, which can be reached directly from the outside by elevators housed in a separate tower. We have here a solution that is straight-forward, convincing, and at the same time antiacademic.

The creation of an office complex that would respond to the demands of the new times within the context of the old Moscow urban fabric was the basic idea leading to the concept of the so-called "sky-hook." **Figs. 22** Moscow is a centralized city, characterized by a number of concentric **23** ring boulevards connected by radial main streets emanating from the Kremlin. The proposal intends to place these structures at the inter-sections of the radials and the boulevards, where the most intense traffic is generated. Everything delivered to the building by horizontal traffic **Plates 2** is subsequently transported vertically by elevator and then redistributed **28** in a horizontal direction.

Compared to the prevalent American high-rise system the innovation consists in the fact that the horizontal (the useful) is clearly separated from the vertical (the support, the necessary). This in turn allows for clarity in the interior layout, which is essential for office structures and is usually predicated by the structural system. The resulting external build-ing volume achieves elementary diversity in all six visual directions.

The problems connected with the development of these building types, including the whole scientific organization of work and business, are being dealt with on an international level. In this field, as in others, our social system will open up new possibilities. In this field, as in others, reconstruction will pose new demands.

The Reconstruction of Industrial Architecture

In the Five-Year State Master Plan for Social Development, industrialization represents the largest single item in the budget. Billions are being given to industry. Patience will be required, since the effects of this reconstruction will become evident only in future years. There is a close connection between industrial planning and the reconstruction of our old, sluggish agriculture. A new term has been introduced—the "wheat factory." With the arrival of the machine, the tractor, and science, 100,000-acre tracts of virgin soil are now being readied for cultivation. This is a leap forward comparable to the transition from the spinning wheel to modern textile industry. The only difference is that the wheat factory is located directly in nature and is most intimately connected with its human settlements. As a result of this development, the architect is now faced with the problem of the new village.

Many new industrial plants are being built, but you may ask "How does this concern the architect? The modern, large industrial plant is an aggregation, a synthetic machine, composed of individual machines. The planning of this composite unit is the task of the engineer. All that remains to be done by the architect is to design the outer shell."

This seemingly logical point of view puts the machine first while forgetting the human being and the human community. Work for the community is not simply a matter of adding up figures; a number of psychophysical components must be included in the final balance. In our country the factory has ceased to exist as a place of exploitation and as a hated institution. Work is the most noble of human activities. Once the term "Palace of Labor" is introduced it should, strictly speaking, refer to the factory. Wages and material gain alone are not enough to stimulate productivity—a new psychological force must take the place of capitalistic competition. Free Socialistic competition, i.e., the competition between individual factories, plants, and trade groups provides such a stimulus. The architectural design of the new environment for work has become an active and important element in this process. By virtue of exact division of time and work rhythm, and by making each individual share in a large common responsibility, the factory has become the real place of education—the university for new Socialist man. Our largest meetings are held in the factories. Stage plays and concerts are performed in large factories during work breaks. Thus, the factory has become the crucible of Socialization for the urban population; its architecture is not merely the wrapping for a complex of machines but something completely new and different.

The New City

Social evolution leads to the elimination of the old dichotomy between city and country. The city endeavors to draw nature right into its center and by means of industrialization to introduce a higher level of culture into the country.

The city of today can no longer satisfy all the demands made on it by society. The conditions out of which old cities developed have long since disappeared, but we continue to live in their petrified shells.

The layout of our old cities was determined by business, trade, and exchange—the marketplace; as well as by protection and defense against war and attack—the castle or the Roman camp. This led to the development of the concentric and the gridiron town plan.

In our day these old systems are supposed to satisfy all kinds of new needs. Twice a day the city experiences its ebb and flood. Traffic has become a major problem. It is increasingly becoming a question of time rather than space. Traffic has to connect all developed parts of the city: business and administration centers, cultural districts, industrial districts, and housing. The social substructure of all these areas has been entirely changed in our country. Departments that deal with organization and design must attack these problems that face the Soviet Union in a new spirit. Specialized knowledge alone—even the best—is inadequate in this situation. Everything must be conceived on the basis of broad concepts and an unshakable confidence in the future. Two basic forces, fundamental to the treatment of the problem of cities, must be taken into consideration: the social structure of society, which allows the new city organism to give the fullest expression to its life processes; and the level of technology on which the realization of these new ideas depends. This ought to lead to the following developments:

(a) City type and urban structure.
(b) Districts within which individual social neighborhoods establish themselves.
(c) The design of the resulting volumes and spaces must take into account the new social and psychophysical characteristics of society.

Several such proposals stand ready to be debated. As first attempts trying to take hold of the subject while searching for some kind of new point of departure, they tend to be of a more or less theoretical nature. However, all these proposals have one thing in common, namely, that the actual realization of such cities is being projected for the final stage of the present transition toward Socialism. On the whole, these planning efforts are intended for flat terrain. It is assumed that these cities already harbor a classless society.

Proposal (a–d) of Fig. 25 develops a metropolis conceived as the **Figs. 24** intellectual and administrative center of a territory. It is based on the **25** assumption that free competition rather than competitive struggle will be the main source of strength of the society of the future.

Three principal long-distance arteries lead to the central railroad station and the airport. The centrally located public core, where all **Plate 57** communal activities take place, includes sports and amusement facilities as well. Three city districts are located in the area between the traffic arteries: the administrative and government centers (intellectual center); the production center; and the educational center.

The proposal is based on the assumption that the population of the city will be in a state of continuous motion: people arrive from the outside, from the country, and return there. In the city itself no one is any longer tied to one and the same occupation. Living quarters are changed with each new employment.

The city originates from three nodal points, which remain eccentrically fixed during the subsequent growth of the city. This eccentricity is a result of the direction of growth into the country and traffic moving on elevated highways in circles.

More than half of the city area is given to green spaces, while residential and communal buildings are provided with landscaping at varying levels.

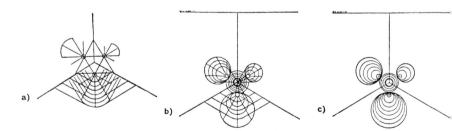

Fig. 24. T. Varentsov: Housing systems for the city of the future.

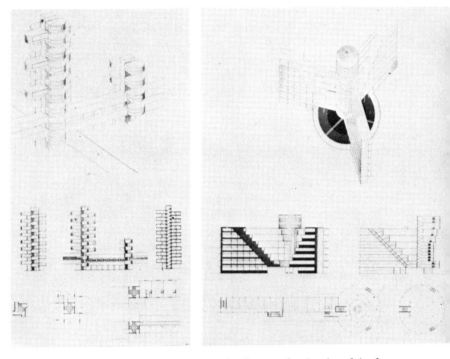

Fig. 25. Varentsov (Vkhutein): Schematic diagrams for the city of the future.

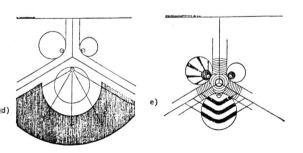

d)

e)

61

Buildings are conceived as standard units according to function. Thus we have high-rise buildings for offices in the government district, and two types of residential buildings: the individual apartment, where **Fig. 24** residence and place of work remain separated; and the commune, in which a community unites to perform all of its activities in one place, so that place of work, club, restaurants, and dwellings are combined into a single complex.

Nowadays we are familiar with two extremes: the metropolis as a concentration of industry, and the village surrounded by agricultural production. In the new type of city system described above, a combination of both these tendencies becomes possible. The territory may be planned either way—the parabolic strips of the drawing accommodate both technical production areas and food supply. This idea is based on **Fig. 25** technical resources already available to us, so that the proposals are **Fig. 25** feasible as far as that is concerned. Only the fact that the whole is supposed to be built as a complete entity—all at once and according to a fixed plan—makes this proposal seem fantastic. But even today new cities are being planned and built as a whole, as for instance Canberra, the capital city of Australia.

We also draw attention to the proposal for a "linear city" based on **Plate 57** a system by Charles Gide. The whole city represents a single street, a spine, whose vertebrae are made up of individual residential blocks.

Another proposal presented here is that of two old cities connected **Fig. 26** by a linear city. As with all problems of the future—and that includes the questions of planning and urbanism—reality will surpass the most daring prophecies. Current discussion is not about details but about the fundamental attitude toward the total character of building development and the principles of design. It is a question of "geometry" versus "organic." It is a question of the social condition of the human society for which one designs. Whenever anarchic and unbridled conflict becomes the basis of a social order, prescribed order tends to act as the only cohesive force, and "geometry" as an ordering system becomes most useful and unequivocal. However, when a community organizes itself into a living organism, with each individual playing his inseparable part, incapable of separate existence, then we believe that we can perceive the basis for the development of a new urban order. How the core of these new urban complexes will develop is a matter of selection and depends on the site conditions and the landscape in which they are to be placed, while their form should develop by organic growth.

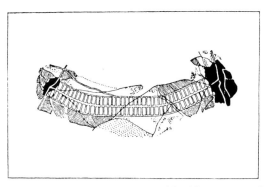

Fig. 26. Schematic diagram showing two old cities connected by a new "linear city."

The Future and Utopia

In these times we must be very objective, very practical, and totally unromantic, so that we can catch up with the rest of the world and overtake it. But we also know that even the best "business" will not of itself advance us to a higher level of culture. The next stage of cultural development will encompass all aspects of life: human productivity and creativity, the most precious faculties of man. And this not in order to accumulate profits for individuals, but to produce works that belong to everybody. If we just consider all the accomplishments of our own generation, we are certainly justified in taking for granted a technology capable of solving all the tasks mentioned earlier. One of our utopian ideas is the desire to overcome the limitations of the substructure, the earthbound. We have developed this idea in a series of proposals (sky-hooks, stadium grandstands, Paris garage). Plates 2 The design of the Lenin Institute on the Lenin Hills in Moscow is 28, 62 based on this idea. The building complex consists of a tower structure Figs. 2 (library for 15 million volumes), low-story buildings with reading 29 rooms and workrooms, and a spherical building (elevated in the air) containing a central reading room for 4,000 users. The latter can be

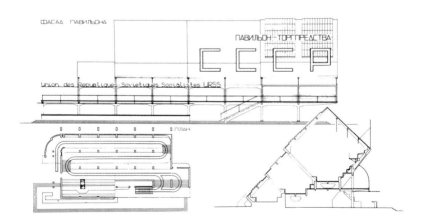

Fig. 27. M. Korgiev: Trade Fair Pavilion for the Paris Commercial Representatives.

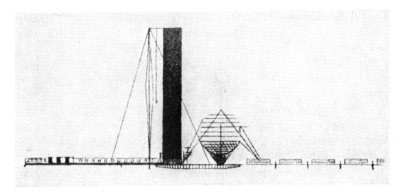

Fig. 28. I. Leonidov: Lenin Institute. Main elevation.

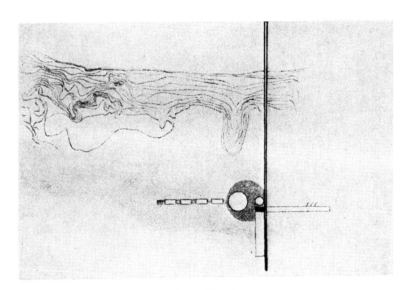

Fig. 29. I. Leonidov: Lenin Institute. Site plan.

65

divided up into several sections, and the sphere itself can be used as a planetarium. The institute is connected to the city across the river by means of an aerotrain.

It is the task of technology to make sure that all these elementary volumes that produce new relationships and tensions in space will be structurally safe.

The idea of the conquest of the substructure, the earthbound, can be extended even further and calls for the conquest of gravity as such. It demands floating structures, a physical-dynamic architecture.

Though in reality a reduction of these futuristic plans and proposals is still necessary, their basic soundness is apparent even at the present time. A good example of this approach is the exhibition building of the Trade Representatives of the USSR in Paris. The designer has taken the "utopia" of the suspended grandstands and developed it **Fig. 27** further to achieve an enclosed building, thereby fusing the path of the visitor with the various objects and goods exhibited. This represents a crystallization of an idea where function, construction, interior space, and exterior volume are intensified by giving the whole a new meaning and a new unity.

Schools of Architecture

We know that the birth of the new architecture will not take place in the schools, and we also know that none of the institutions concerned with design or with actual construction proceed in a truly creative manner. So far we have not been able to develop stable systems responsive to the needs of our time that would embrace the whole building process—starting with design and ending with actual work on the site.

Reconstruction has placed heavy demands on architecture, thus creating a need for a great number of new specialists in this field. Even in most recent times the architectural schools merely *taught* students the technical subjects, whereas they *educated* them in the artistic subjects. This luxury, which places all emphasis on the teaching talents of the master, can no longer be tolerated in our time. We demand a firm, scientific foundation for the *learning* of the art of architecture. The architectural faculty of the Technical Arts Institute (Vkhutein) has acted as the central clearing house in the continuing search for new fundamental concepts that will form the theoretical basis of the new architecture.

Through the initiative of Ladovski, a psychotechnical laboratory was established, charged with the development of proper methods for testing the students' psychotechnical aptitude for architecture.

The design problems given to the students by the school were closely related to the current building programs of the various communes and other state institutions. This represents a source from which the future architect and builder may continuously extract new ideas. Thus the schools, which have often been accused of "utopianism," become the real pace setters in the art of building.

We know the danger inherent in schools. As long as the designer deals only with a sheet of paper, his main driving force will be diligence, competition, and the record performance for which he fights with his school colleagues. This alone can only lead to a new academicism, isolated from life. Because of this, it is necessary to steel youth by simultaneously exposing it to the struggle with real materials and the work of actual construction on the building site. Hence, the new school program allots more and more time to practical work in the field. In this way, and in accordance with the general educational goals to be achieved, the schools must be perpetually concerned with their own reconstruction.

Ideological Superstructure

Let us review some aspects of the life process introduced into our world by the Revolution which, as I write this, is scarcely five years old. During this period the great challenges posed by the cultural revolution have taken deep root in the consciousness of our new generation of architects. It has become obvious to the architect that by virtue of his work he is taking an active part in the building of a new world. For us the work of an artist has no value "as such;" it does not represent an end in itself; it has no intrinsic beauty. The value of a work of art in our society is determined by its relationship to the community. In the creation of each great work of art the contribution of the architect is explicit, while the contribution of the community is latent. The artist, or the creative worker, invents nothing; there is no such thing as divine inspiration. Thus we understand by the term "reconstruction" the conquest of the unresolved, of the "mysterious," and the chaotic.

In our architecture, as in our entire life, we are striving to create social order, i.e., to raise the instinctive to a conscious level.

The ideological superstructure protects and secures work. The socio-economic reconstruction, mentioned earlier, represents the substructure of the renewal that has to be accomplished in architecture. It provides a definite point of departure, but it would be fallacious to account for all the complex interrelationships in such a simple way. Life, organic growth, represents a dialectic process that simultaneously affirms both the yes (plus) and the no (minus). Growth is part of the social life process as well as the result of certain actualities, both affecting the formation of future intentions. On the basis of the existing, an ideology is formed representing a definite view of life and leading to certain interpretations and interrelationships which, in turn, affect further growth. The development of our architecture reflects this dialectical process:

1. *Destruction of tradition*. Material production is stopped in the country. The thirst for superproduction. First design dreams. Subsequent formation of an ideology embodying two basic demands concerning the entire future development: the elementary and invention. A work which is to be in harmony with our time must include invention within its totality. Our time demands designs that have their origin in

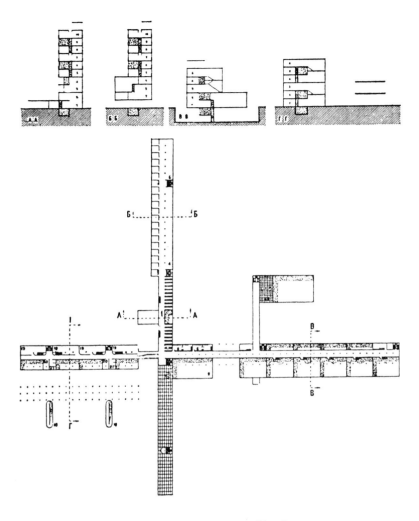

Fig. 30. Building Committee of the R.S.F.S.R.: Housing commune.

elementary forms (geometry). The struggle with the aesthetic of chaos takes its course. The demand is for a conscious order.

2. *Start of construction.* First in industry and production. The concrete situation leads to conflict. Yet the new generation, which has grown up in a time that lacked architecture, does not have sufficient practical experience, has little authority, and has not yet become academic. In the struggle for building commissions the thrust of their ideology is in the direction of basic utilitarian considerations and the satisfaction of basic needs. The slogans are: "constructivism," "functionalism," "engineer" equals "architect." At any rate, whether one said "machine" or "architecture," it was assumed that a solution could be derived from the same algebraic formula, a formula in which the only "unknown" was simply some X to be found by one and the same method. For both the architect and the engineer the result was supposed to work out automatically. It was thought that one need only introduce new structural methods and new materials, and the product would turn out to be a self-evident whole.

3. The first phase of reconstruction demands the concentration of all forces in the sphere of the socio-economic revolution so as to intensify the cultural revolution. The physical, psychological, and emotional factors of a great culture are indivisible. The intrinsic nature of art reveals itself through ordering, organizing, and activating consciousness by emotional energy charges. Architecture is considered pre-eminent among the other arts, and the attention of the community focuses on it. Architectural questions become questions of concern to the masses. The design dreams of the initial period lose their individual character and obtain a firm social basis. The "utilitarians" are once more challenged by the "formalists." The latter assert that architecture is not synonymous with engineering. To solve the utilitarian, the useful, and the expedient, and to construct a volume that functions well for a particular purpose, represents only one part of the problem. In addition, materials must be organized correctly, and the problem of construction must be solved. However, in order to achieve a true work of architecture the whole must be conceived and must come alive as a spatial idea, as well as be a creative effort exerting a definite influence on the human spirit. For this reason it is not enough to be "modern"; on the contrary, it is necessary for the architect as an artist to gain command of all the means of expression that relate to the art of building.

Let us summarize these three points more concisely:

(a) The rejection of art as a mere emotional, individualistic, and romantic affair.

(b) "Objective" work, undertaken with the silent hope that the end product will nevertheless eventually be regarded as a work of art.

(c) Consciously goal-directed work in architecture, which will have a concise artistic effect on the basis of well-prepared objective-scientific criteria.

Such an architecture will actively raise the general standard of living. This represents the dialectic of our development process, which purports to arrive at the affirmative by negation—a process similar to melting down old iron and forging it into new steel.

Moscow, October 1929   El Lissitzky

Plate 1. El Lissitzky: Proun (City), 1920.

Plate 2. K. Malevich: Suprematist Architectonics, 1923.

Plate 3. V. Tatlin: Monument to the Third International. Side elevation. 1920.

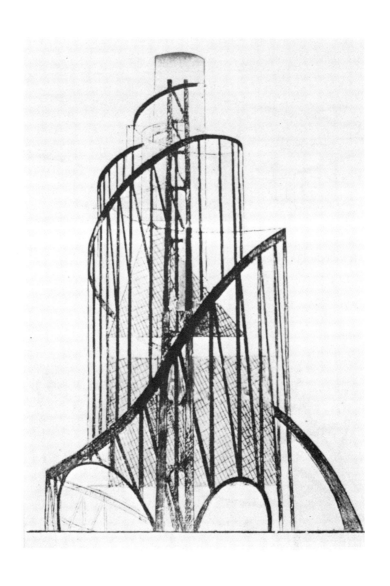

Plate 4. V. Tatlin: Monument to the Third International. Front elevation.

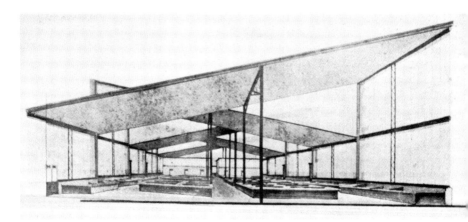

Plate 5. J. Volodko (Vkhutein); Atelier V. Krinski: Market hall, 1923.

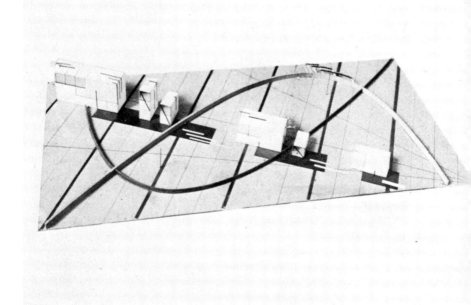

Plate 6. M. Turkus (Vkhutein); Atelier N. Ladovski: Rhythm and movement, 1923.

Plate 7. Atelier N. Ladovski: Restaurant on a cliff, 1922.

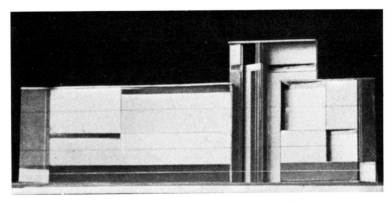

Plate 8. Vkhutein: Basic theory. Surface arrangement, 1927.

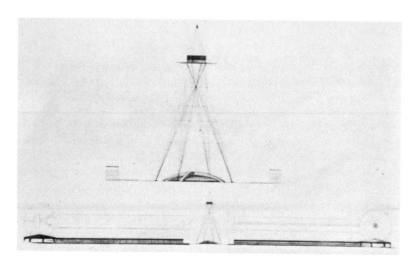

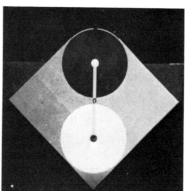

Plate 9. V. Balikhin (Vkhutein): Airport, 1924.

Plate 10. Lopatin (Vkhutein); Atelier N. Ladovski: Skyscraper for the city of Moscow, 1923.
▶

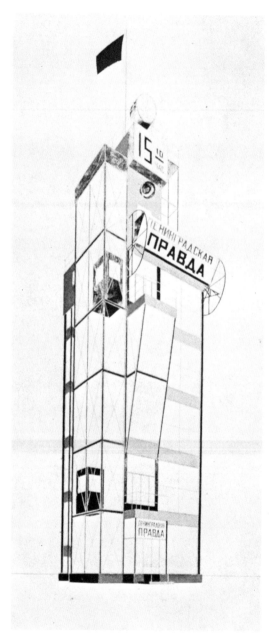

Plate 11.
Brothers Vesnin:
Newspaper building,
1923.

Plate 12.
Brothers Vesnin:
Palace of Labor,
1923. ▶

Plate 13. K. Melnikov: Design for USSR Pavilion in Paris, 1925.

Plate 14. K. Melnikov: USSR Pavilion in Paris, 1925. ▶

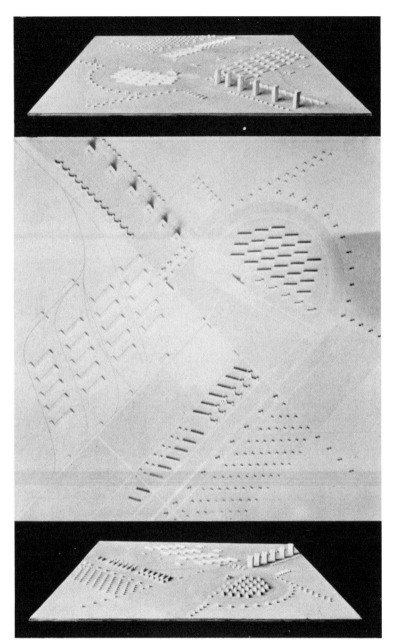

84

Plate 16. Apartment building constructed by Mossoviet.

Plate 15. N. Ladovski: Housing project for the labor commune "Kostino,"
◄   1927.

Plate 17. Kochar (Vkhutein): Housing project.

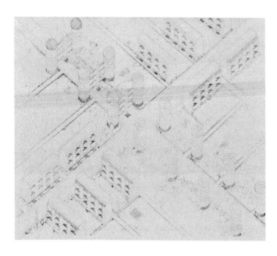

86

Plate 18. M. Ginsburg: Apartments in Moscow.

Plate 19. Atelier Lissitzky (Vkhutein): Village club.

Plate 20. I. Lamtsov: Club for the center of a settlement.

Plate 21. I. Leonidov: Club and planetarium.

Plate 22. Gegello and Krichevskii: Seating arrangement in the House of Culture, Leningrad.

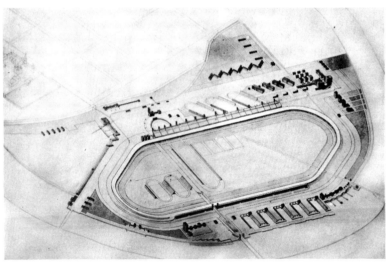

Plate 24. Atelier A. Nikolski: Stadium grandstand, Leningrad. ▶

92

Plate 25. Atelier A. Nikolski: Bathhouse.

Plate 26. Bunin (Vkhutein): Spa hotel on the Black Sea.

Plate 27. El Lissitzky: Sky-hook, aerial view, 1924.

Plate 28. El Lissitzky: Sky-hook, 1924.

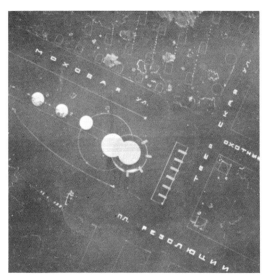

Plate 29.
N. Travin (Vkhutein):
Congress center.

Plate 30. M. Ginsburg: Government buildings for Alma-Ata. Various views.

Plate 31. Offices of the Supreme Economic Council in Kharkov.

Plate 32. Offices of the Supreme Economic Council in Kharkov.

Plate 33. A. Zilchenko: Offices for the Central Industrial Administration.

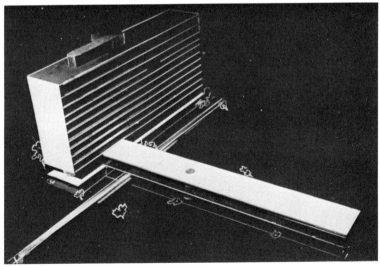

Plate 34. I. Leonidov: Office building for the Union of Cooperatives.

Plate 35. B. Velikovski: Gostorg offices, Moscow.

Plate 36.
B. Velikovski:
Gostorg.

Plate 37. B. Velikovski: Gostorg.

Plate 38. B. Velikovski: Gostorg. Staircase.

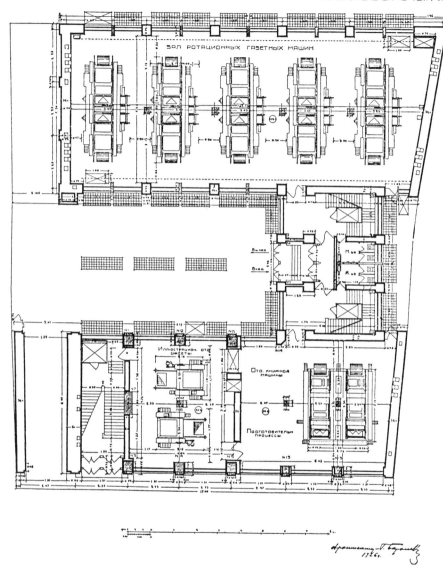

Plate 39. G. Barkhin: Plan of the *Izvestia* Building.

Plate 40. G. Barkhin: *Izvestia* Building. First design proposal. ▶

Plate 41. G. Barkhin: *Izvestia* Building.

Plate 42. G. Barkhin: *Izvestia* Building. Details.

Plate 43. S. Chernichev: Lenin Institute, Moscow.

Plate 44. S. Chernichev: Lenin Institute, Moscow.

Plate 45. Brothers Vesnin: Department Store.

Plate 46. Brothers Vesnin: Department store. Entrance detail.

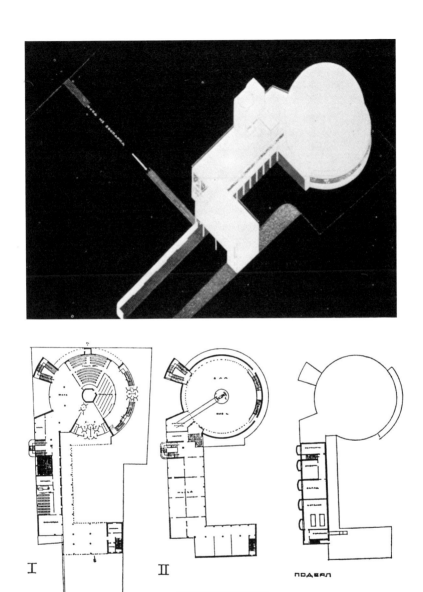

I II ПОДВАЛ

Plate 47. M. Barsht and M. Ssiniavski: Planetarium, Moscow.

Plate 48. Cupola assembly for the Moscow Planetarium.

Plate 49. K. Melnikov, architect; Shukhov, engineer: Bus garage, Moscow.

116

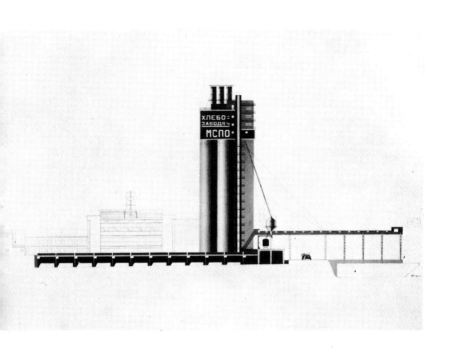

Plate 50. Mostakov (Vkhutein): Bread factory.

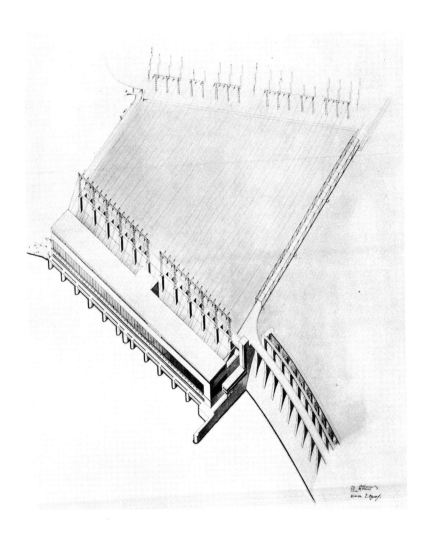

Plate 51. Hydroelectric power plant, Dniepropetrovsk. Design proposal by the Architectural Department of the Chief Construction Office. Architect: V. Vesnin; collaborators: N. Kolli, G. Orlov, S. Andreev-ski.

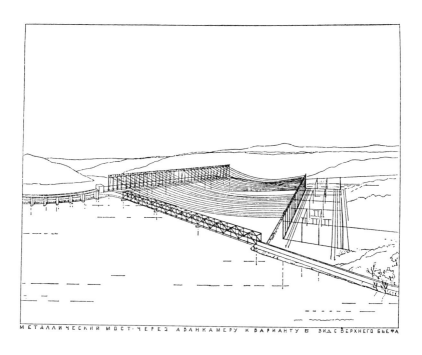

МЕТАЛЛИЧЕСКИЙ МОСТ-ЧЕРЕЗ АВАНКАМЕРУ К ВАРИАНТУ В ВИД С ВЕРХНЕГО БЬЕФА

Plate 52. Hydroelectric power plant, Dniepropetrovsk. Design proposal by the Architectural Department of the Chief Construction Office. Architect: V. Vesnin; collaborators: N. Kolli, G. Orlov, S. Andreevski.

Plate 53. Nikolaev and Fissenko: Institute of Science.

Plate 54. V. Vesnin: Institute of Mineralogy. ▶

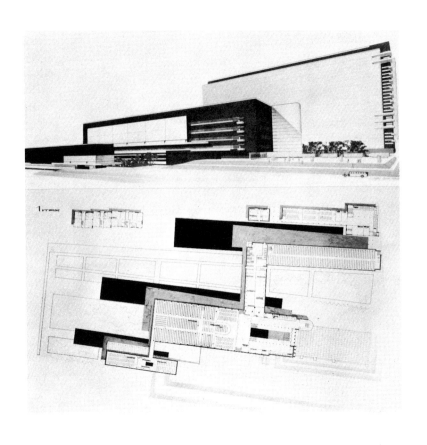

Plate 55. D. Fridman, W. Fridman, D. Markov: Lenin Library in Moscow.
Competition design.

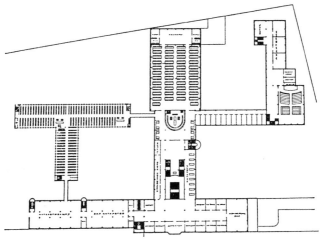

Plate 56. Brothers Vesnin: Lenin Library in Moscow. Competition design.

Plate 57. T. Varentsov (Vkhutein): Utopian city.

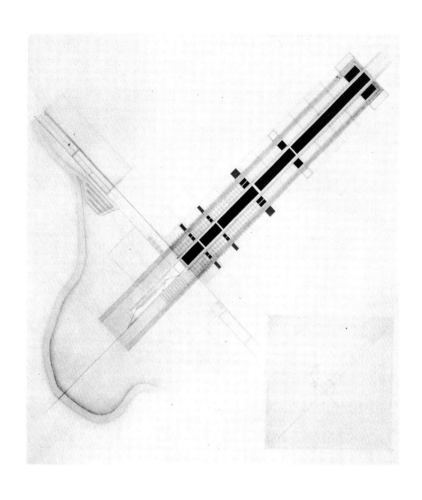

Plate 58. B. Lavrov (Vkhutein): Linear city.

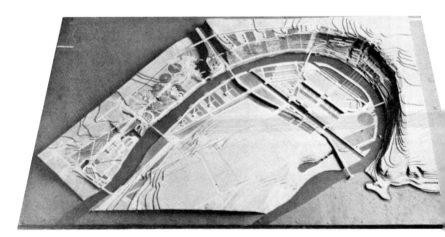

Plate 59. L. Saleskaia (Vkhutein): Park of Culture and Recreation in Moscow. General layout.

Plate 60. I. Leonidov: Lenin Institute.

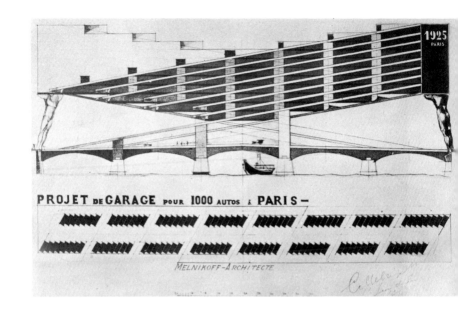

Plate 61. K. Melnikov: Design for a large parking garage in Paris.

Plate 62. K. Melnikov: Club in Moscow.

Appendix

Foreword

The following articles and illustrations are meant to complement the translation of El Lissitzky's report on "The Reconstruction of Architecture in the Soviet Union" of 1929 in two respects:

Parts I and II of the Appendix supply a biography of Lissitzky and are further intended to provide an insight into the evolution of his artistic and theoretical ideas on the basis of selected essays written during the years 1921 to 1926, that characterize his "transfer from painting to architecture," a subject that was given its final expression in the preceding material on the theme: The New Architecture in Russia. Even while his report was being published in Vienna, Lissitzky and his collaborators were being confronted by steadily growing counterforces. This aspect is explained in the articles of Part III of the Appendix. The last, anonymous, article is in fact already more or less an outline of the architectural doctrines that eventually became prevalent throughout the Stalin era, and quite possibly represents the last report on Soviet architecture in a German publication during the Hitler period. One cannot help but admire the courage of Joseph Gantner—now Professor of Art History in Basel—who in 1929 was the first to publish the original Lissitzky text, and who in 1933 dared to tackle this subject once more in the publication *Die Neue Stadt*.

The third part of the Appendix is not merely meant to illustrate the final chapter of modern architecture in Russia but should be viewed as an additional attempt to familiarize the reader with the background from which Lissitzky's book emanated. The selection of the articles and travel reports was made solely for this purpose, and in no way represents an attempt to describe in a documentary fashion the peaceful invasion of Russia by German city planners and architects under the leadership of Ernst May. These pieces were chosen because of their graphic vividness and great relevance to the subject.

Dieter Helms was helpful in the compilation of the Appendix by virtue of his valuable preliminary work in 1962 for the catalogue for the exhibition *The Twenties in Hanover*.

Ulrich Conrads

133

I. Biography

El Lissitzky*

(El = Eleazar Marcovich), born near Smolensk in 1890, of a Jewish middle-class family. Studied at the Technische Hochschule in Darmstadt from 1909 to 1914, and returned to Russia shortly before the war. In 1917 he completed his architectural degree in Moscow, and it is assumed that he was active as an artist from 1912 onward, initially as an illustrator of books in the manner of Chagall. The latter, who at that time held the post of Commissar of Fine Arts in the gubernatorial district of Vitebsk, in 1917 put Lissitzky on the staff of the Academy of Arts in that city. There Lissitzky met Malevich and probably also Tatlin, both of whom exerted considerable influence on his subsequent work. In 1919 he held the first exhibition of his Proun work. In 1920 he went to Düsseldorf to found a constructivist movement, and 1921 he became professor at the Moscow Academy of Arts. After the proclamation of Lenin's edict against the avant-garde, Lissitzky left the USSR for Germany (Berlin and Hanover) and Switzerland. The following years mark his literary cooperation with van Doesburg, Mies van der Rohe, Werner Gräff, and Kurt Schwitters. In 1922, in cooperation with Ilya Ehrenburg, Lissitzky published the magazine *Veshch* (*Object*) in Berlin. Only three issues came out. In 1923 he designed the *Proun-Space* in the Great Berlin Art Exhibition; he also published the folio of figurines for the play *Victory Over the Sun* in Hanover. From 1923 on he repeatedly went to Davos for treatment of tuberculosis. At that time he met Sophie Küppers, Paul Erich Küppers' widow, whom he later married. In 1925 the *Kunstismen* (*Art-isms*) written in collaboration with Hans Arp were published. In 1926 he designed the Room of the Abstractionists of the International Art Exhibition in Dresden, followed by the Cabinet of the Abstractionists in the Hanover Provincial Museum, designed in 1927. In 1928 he designed the Russian section of the Newspaper Exhibition in Cologne. In 1928–29 he returned to Russia. In 1930 he published *Russia—The Reconstruction of Architecture in the Soviet Union*. He died in 1941 in the USSR of his lung ailment.

---

* From the exhibition catalogue *The Twenties in Hanover*, p. 208, published by the Kunstverein Hannover e. V., Hanover, 1962.

II. El Lissitzky: Programmatic Essays and Work Commentaries 1921–1926

El Lissitzky: The Plastic Organization of the Electro-Mechanical Show *Victory over the Sun**

The work in question is the fragment of an effort that originated in Moscow 1920–21. Here—as in all of my work—I do not merely strive to reform an existing situation, but, quite to the contrary, I make it my goal to create a completely new way of looking at things.

No one seems to pay any attention to the magnificent spectacle of our cities, simply because "everyone" has become part and parcel of the spectacle himself. Each particular energy is harnessed to its own individual purpose. The whole is amorphous. All energies must be organized to achieve unity; they have to be channeled and made apparent. The result is a piece of work—you may call it a work of art. We intend to erect a scaffolding in a square, accessible and open from all directions. The scaffolding represents the stage machinery of the show designed to provide the objects of the show with multitudinous possibilities of movement. In order to accomplish this, the individual parts must be movable, turnable, stretchable, etc. The transition from one level to the next must be accomplished with ease. Skeleton construction should be used throughout so as not to obscure the moving objects during the show. The objects themselves are to be designed as required or desired. They slide, roll, and hover on, in, and above the scaffolding. All show objects are brought into motion by means of electro-mechanical forces and devices, with central control in the hands of a single individual who acts as the director of the whole show. His place is in the center of the scaffolding at the energy-control panels. He controls all movement, sound, and light. At the flick of a switch the sound system is turned on and the whole place may suddenly reverberate with the din of a railroad station, or the roar of Niagara Falls, or the pounding of a steel-rolling mill. The director gives the show objects a voice by speaking into a microphone connected to an arc-lamp or

---

* Preface to a folio of ten lithographs of figurines, published in 1923 in Hanover.

136

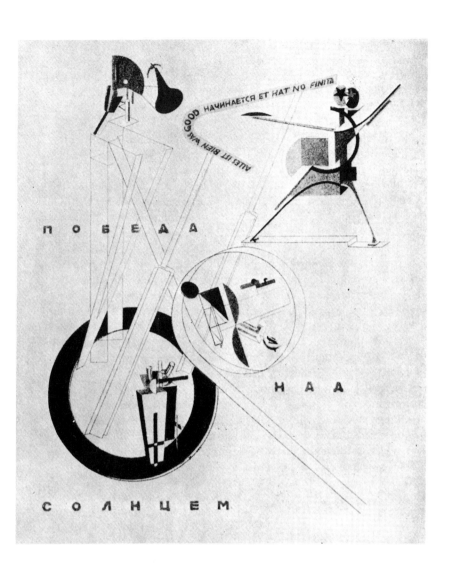

Fig. 31. El Lissitzky: Part of stage machinery for the plastic organization of the electro-mechanical show *Victory Over the Sun*, 1920/21.

some other device which, in turn, may be designed to modify his voice **Fig. 31** in accordance with the respective character of each of the individual figurines. Electrical sentences flash and dim. Light rays, diffused by prisms and reflectors, follow the movements of the figurines in the play. By such means the most elementary processes are intensified to maximum effect by the director.

For the opening performance of the electro-mechanical show I chose a contemporary work, in spite of the fact that it was written for the traditional stage, namely, the futurist opera *Victory Over the Sun* by A. Kruchonikh, the inventor of the sound poem and leader of the avant-garde in Russian poetry. The opera was performed for the first time in 1913 in Petersburg. The music was composed by Matiushin (quarter tones). Malevich painted the decorations (the curtain = a black square).

The sun as the expression of old world energy is torn down from the heavens by modern man, who by virtue of his technical superiority creates his own energy source. The idea of the opera is woven into a simultaneity of happenings. Speech is alogical. Individual songs are in the form of sound poems.

The text of the opera has forced me to preserve some resemblance to parts of the human anatomy for my figurines. The colors of the individual parts of these panels should be regarded as material-equivalents, similar to my Proun work. In other words, during the performance the red, yellow, or black parts of the figurines will not be painted with these colors but will be made of their corresponding genuine material counterparts: such as polished copper, dull iron, etc. I have left to others the further elaboration and application of the ideas and forms put down here in order to address myself to new tasks.

El Lissitzky: PROUN SPACE,
The Great Berlin Art Exhibition of 1923*

Proun : see "MOSCOW 1919," "MA," "De Stijl" 1922, Vol. 6.

Space : That which is not looked at through a keyhole, nor through an open door. Space does not exist for the eye only: it is not a picture; one wants to live in it.

---

* From: *G 1*, edited by Gräff and Lissitzky, published by H. Richter, Berlin, July 1923.

Fig. 32. PROUN SPACE.

Among all of the junk displayed in the exhibition hall of the Lehrt Railroad Station, various boxlike "spaces" have been integrated. One of these boxes has kindly been put at my disposal. Given were the six surfaces (floor, four walls, ceiling); they are to be designed, but, mind you, not as a living room, for there is an exhibition going on. In an exhibition people keep walking all around. Thus, space has to be organized in such a way as to impel everyone automatically to perambulate in it.

The first form designed to "pull in" a person coming from the great hall is placed diagonally, "directing" the visitor toward the large horizontal of the front wall, and from there to wall No. 3 with a vertical. At the exit—STOP! i.e., a square at the bottom—the basic
Fig. 32 element of all design. A relief on the ceiling, placed within the same visual angle, repeats this movement. The floor design was not realized due to reasons of economy.

The space (as exhibition space) was designed by using elementary forms and materials: line, surface and rod, cube, sphere, black, white, grey, and wood; in addition, surfaces were applied flat to the walls (color), and other surfaces were placed at right angles to the walls (wood). The two reliefs on the walls provide the theme and focus for all the wall surfaces. (The cube on the left wall is juxtaposed to the sphere on the front wall and, in turn, is placed in juxtaposition to the rod on the right wall.) This space is not a living room. The preceding description has revealed the axes of my space design. By means of this example I wish to elucidate a set of principles that I consider necessary for the basic organization of any space. On the basis of this given real space I shall make an attempt to clarify these principles, taking into account the fact that we are dealing here with an exhibiton showroom, i.e., a demonstration space.

139

Thus, the organization of the wall cannot be conceived as anything like a representative picture-painting. Whether one "paints" on a wall or whether one hangs pictures on it, both actions are equally wrong. New space neither needs nor demands pictures—it is not a picture transposed on a surface. This explains the painters' hostility toward us: we are destroying the wall as the resting place for their pictures. If one *wants* to produce the illusion of life in a closed room, one should proceed as follows: hang a sheet of glass on the wall and instead of putting canvas behind it, attach a periscopic device which will at each instant reproduce real events in real colors and in real motion.

I am aiming at a spatial equilibrium, both mobile and elementary, that will not be upset by the introduction of a telephone or a piece of standardized office furniture. *Space exists for man—man does not exist for space.* The cubic footage required by man for rest, work, and social intercourse must be brought into harmony, and this harmony must be brought into motion by means of an elementary structural system that will respond to his various needs and requirements. *We reject space as a painted coffin for our living bodies.*

The Hague, May 1923   El Lissitzky

1924

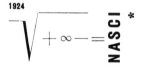

ENOUGH of MACHINE
         MACHINE
         MACHINE
         MACHINE
once modern art production has been reached.

The machine is nothing but a brush—and indeed a very primitive one—by means of which the canvas of the world is being painted. All

---

* From: *Kunstismen*, March 8/9, April/July 1924; Vol. 2, No. 8/9. This double issue appeared under the editorial direction of El Lissitzky and Kurt Schwitters.
"Nature, from Latin *nasci*, i.e., becoming, or emerging into being, includes everything that develops, forms, or moves on the basis of its own strength." Dictionary definition.

tools set into motion are forces directed toward the crystallization of amorphous nature—in fact this is the goal of nature itself.

To prove that one can write with a quill dipped in one's own blood in the age of the typewriter is an unproductive waste of time, to say the least. And to prove today that the task of all design—including art—is not *re*-presentation but *pre*-sentation, is equally a waste of time.

The machine has not divorced us from nature. By means of the machine we have discovered a new, previously unanticipated feature of nature.

Modern art has arrived by entirely intuitive and independent means at the same results as modern science. Modern art, like modern science, has reduced form to its basic elements in order to reassemble them again according to the universal laws of nature. In this process both have arrived at the same formula:

EACH FORM IS THE FROZEN TEMPORARY IMAGE OF A PROCESS. THUS, ANY WORK MERELY REPRESENTS A WAY STATION IN THE PROCESS OF BECOMING, AND NOT A FROZEN GOAL.

We recognize works that incorporate a specific system, but it must be a system that has become conscious during the work process, and not before.

We wish to design for repose, i.e., the repose of nature, where tremendous tensions keep even the rotation of the planets in equilibrium.

Our work is not philosophy, neither is it a system relating to a specific theory of nature; it is part of nature and must therefore itself be regarded as an object of knowledge.

All this represents an attempt that points toward a collective purpose which is beginning to influence all contemporary national art production. It is still a civil war of contradictions. Today, this civil war is being fought for the survival of art as such.

In the year 1924 the square root–$\sqrt{}$–will emerge from the infinite –∞–oscillating between the meaningful–$+$–and the meaningless–$-$– called: NASCI.

El Lissitzky, Locarno, Hospital

El Lissitzky: A. and Pangeometry*

After all, seeing is also an A.
(Abbreviations: A. = Art, F. = Form)

In the period between 1918 and 1921 a lot of old rubbish was destroyed. In Russia too we have torn A. from its holy pedestal "while spitting on its altar" (Malevich 1915). During the first Dada happening in Zurich, A. was proclaimed "magic crap" and man "the measure of all tailors" (Arp).

For instance now, after 5 years (5 centuries according to the old reckoning of time), Grosz in Germany reproaches himself for one thing only: "We made one single mistake, which is to take A. seriously in the first place." However, a few lines further on he writes: "Hence, the question whether my work should be called A. largely depends on the question of whether the future will belong to the working classes." The latter is my conviction, aside from the fact that beliefs, crap, and tailors do not represent universal A. criteria. The term A. resembles a chemist's graduated glass. Each age contributes its own quantity: for example, 5 drams of the perfume "Coty" to tickle the nostrils of the fine gentry. Or another example, 10 cc of sulfuric acid to be thrown into the face of the ruling classes. Or, 15 cc of some kind of metallic solution that later changes into a new source of light. Thus, A. is an invention of the mind, i.e., a complex, where rationality is fused with imagination, the physical with the mathematical, the $\sqrt{1}$ with $\sqrt{-1}$. The series of analogies I shall present below are not offered as proof—my work serves that purpose much better—but in order to clarify my views. Parallels between A. and mathematics must be drawn very carefully, for any overlap is fatal for A.

Planimetric Space

Plastic F.—like mathematics—begins with counting. Its space is made up of physical, two-dimensional, flat surfaces. Its rhythm, the elementary harmony of the natural numerical series 1, 2, 3, 4 ... .

* From: *Europa Almanach*, Painting, Literature, Music, Architecture, Sculpture, Stage, Film, Fashion, and containing some residual observations of no less importance. Edited by C. Einstein, P. Westheim. Potsdam, Gustav Kiepenheuer Verlag, 1925.

The newly created object (the A. object is the product of a copulation between the natural object and the object in which the work is being realized, as described in the paragraph "The A. object"), let's say a relief, is compared with real objects in nature. For example, if the relief shows the front part of an animal hiding part of another animal behind, this then does not mean that the latter, the hidden part, has ceased to exist; it simply means that a certain distance exists between the two objects—a space. As a consequence, through experience the knowledge is gained that distance exists between objects and that objects exist *in space*.

Thus, the two-dimensional plane ceases to be merely a surface. The plane begins to include space, and the mathematical series 1, ·1 ½, 2, 2 ½ ... is created.

Perspective Space

The simple flat surface perceived by the eye stretches and extends into vivid space, evolving into a new system. The perspective mode finds its expression within this system. It is commonly assumed that perspective representation of space is objective, unequivocal, and obvious. People say, "The camera too sees the world in terms of perspective," but this ignores the fact that, contrary to common practice in the West, the Chinese have built a camera with concave rather than convex lenses, thereby producing an equally objective image of the world in the mechanical sense, but obviously quite different in all other respects. Perspective representation of space is based on a rigid three-dimensional view of the world based on the laws of Euclidean geometry. The world is put into a cubic box and transformed within the picture plane into something resembling a pyramidal form. (During the Renaissance one-point perspective was most commonly used and highly developed, the cube being represented by placing it parallel to our face. This is a façade view of the world, where depth becomes a stage viewed statically, which is why at that time perspective and stage design had so much in common.) Here, the apex of the visual cone has its location either in our eye, i.e., in front of the object, or is projected to the horizon, i.e., behind the object. The former approach has been taken by the East, the latter by the West.

Perspective limits space; it has made it finite, closed. However, despite all of this, the "sum total" (here "sum total" means the aggregate of all possible numbers that may be geometrically expressed by a straight line—"the fixed line") of A. has been enriched in the sense that each point, even one infinitely close, can be represented by a number. Planimetric space has produced the arithmetic series. In it, objects are perceived according to the relationship 1, 2, 3, 4, 5 .... Perspective space resembles a geometric series, and objects are perceived according to the relationship 1, 2, 4, 8, 16, 32 .... Until our time the "sum total" of A. has not experienced any new extensions. However, a fundamental reorientation has taken place in science. The geocentric cosmic order of Ptolemy has been replaced by the heliocentric order of Copernicus. Rigid Euclidean space has been destroyed by Lobachevski, Gauss, and Rieman. The impressionists were the first artists who began to explode traditional perspective space. The methods of the cubists were even more radical. They pulled the space-confining horizon into the foreground and identified it with the surface of the painting. They built up the solid surface of the canvas by means of psychological devices (pasted-on wall tapestries, etc.) and by elementary destruction of form. They built from the plane of the picture forward into space. The ultimate results of this process: Picasso's reliefs and the contrereliefs of Tatlin.

The Italian futurists used a different approach. They moved the tip of the visual cone outside of the eye. They did not want to stand in front of the object but to stand in it. They fragmented the single perspective center and scattered the pieces over the whole plane of the picture. However, they failed to bring this process to its logical conclusion: the tools of the painter are inadequate for that purpose, the photographic camera would have to be used.

The establishment of the ☐ by K. Malevich (Petersburg 1913) was the first manifestation of the extension of the "sum total" of A. (Mondrian accomplished the ultimate solution in the development of Western painting. He reduces surface to its primeval state, namely surface *only*, in the sense that there is no longer any spatial in or out of a given surface. Whenever Mondrian's principle is transposed by fashionable A.'s onto the three surfaces of a room, it turns into decoration.)

Our numerical system, being a positional system, has been making use of 0 for a long time, but only in the sixteenth century did 0 first cease to be regarded as "nothing," and become a numeral (Cordano, Tartaglia), i.e., a real number. And only now, in the twentieth century, has the ☐ been recognized as a plastic quantity, i.e., the 0 of the total body of A. This fully chromatic, fully color-saturated ☐ on a white surface has begotten a new conception of space.

New optical experience has taught us that two surfaces of different intensity must be conceived as having a varying distance relationship between them, even though they may lie in the same plane.

Irrational Space

Strictly speaking, distances in this space are measured only by the intensity and the position of rigidly defined color planes. Such space is structured within a framework of the most unequivocal directions: vertically, horizontally, or diagonally. It is a positional system. These distances cannot be measured with a finite scale, as for instance objects in planimetric or perspective space. Here distances are irrational and cannot be represented as a finite relationship of two whole numbers.

An example of such irrationality is the relationship of the diagonal of a square to its side, i.e., $= \sqrt{2} = 1.4$, or more precisely, 1.41, or still more precisely, 1.414, etc., becoming increasingly more accurate, *ad infinitum*.

Suprematism has extended the apex of the finite visual cone of perspective into infinity.

It has broken through the "blue lampshade of the heavens." The color of space is no longer assumed to be a single *blue* ray of the color spectrum, but the whole spectrum—*white*. Suprematist space can be formed in front of the surface as well as in depth. If one assigns the value 0 to the picture surface, then one may call the depth direction − (negative), and the frontal direction + (positive), or vice versa. Thus, suprematism has swept away the illusion of three-dimensional space on a plane, replacing it by the ultimate illusion of *irrational* space with attributes of infinite extensibility in depth and foreground.

This brings us to an A. complex that can be brought into juxtaposition with the mathematical analogy of an uninterrupted straight line, containing the whole natural numerical series which embraces: whole, decimal, negative, positive, and irrational numbers, including 0.

However, that is not all. Mathematics has created a "new thing": imaginary (imaginary = not real, assumed) numbers. These include numbers which, when multiplied by themselves, result in negative values. The square root of the negative of 1 is an imaginary thing called i ($\sqrt{-1} = i$). We now enter a realm that cannot be directly registered by the senses, that cannot be demonstrated, that follows from a purely logical construction and therefore represents an elementary crystallization of human thought. What does this have to do with sense perception, or simple vividness in A.? In their vital quest for the enlargement of F. in A., a number of modern artists—including some of my friends—believe that they can build up multidimensional real spaces that may be entered without an umbrella, where space and time have been combined into a mutually interchangeable single whole. Concurrently with this, they relate their theories with an altogether much too agile superficiality to the most advanced scientific theories, without having a genuinely deep understanding of these theories (viz., multidimensional space, theory of relativity, Minkowski's universe, etc.). Now the productive artist should certainly be allowed to expound any theory he wishes, provided his work remains positive. In our field, only the direction of expansion has been positive up to now, but because of incorrect interpretations of seductive scientific theories the works themselves remain inadequate. The revolutionary concepts of the new world of mathematics are not only seductive to plastic F. Earlier, Lobachevsky had already exploded absolute Euclidean space. On the basis of terrestrial scale relationships, Euclid constructed a *mathematical* space that knows no curvature, and that is therefore capable of receiving a square on the surface. This, in turn, allows us to measure the square on the basis of a *fixed* scale. Using the square as a base, a cube can be constructed accordingly. Lobachevsky and Gauss were the first to prove that Euclidean space represents only one case among an infinite number of other spaces. However, our senses are incapable of visualizing these spaces, as opposed to mathematics, which by its very nature operates independently of our senses. It follows that the mathematically existing multidimensional spaces really cannot be visualized, neither can they be represented; in short, it is impossible to give them material form. We can only change the form of our physical space but not its structure, i.e., its three-dimensionality. We cannot change the degree of curvature of our space in a real way, i.e., the square or the cube cannot be transformed into any other stable form. Only a mirage may be capable of giving us such an illusion. The theory of relativity has provided evidence that quantities of time and space are dependent on the motion of each respective system. According to this theory, a man may die even before he was born. However, insofar as actual pragmatic sense-experience teaches us, things move the other way, forcing us to follow our own physical laws and building up A. F.'s which must needs affect us through the medium of our five physical senses.

In terms of a new component of plastic F., time should be considered first. In the studios of the modern artists it is believed that a unity of time and space—both interchangeable—can be created. But time and space are really two different species. The space of our physical and perceptual environment is three-dimensional. It is quite impossible for any one of us to meander up, down, right, or left in time, our time is one-dimensional. A clear distinction must be made between three-dimensional physical space and multidimensional mathematical spaces. There is only *one* time—in physics as well as in mathematics. We know of no space divorced from objects and vice versa. To create space means to create objects. Objects can be divided into elements. Time is continuous; it cannot be divided into elements. Space is *divergent*; time is *sequential*. We have to be clear about this to understand what follows.

Our senses have certain natural capacities that may be heightened by technical means. So far, this merely represents an extension of our sense capacities, not yet a fundamental transformation of the sense ratios.

For example, our visual space has a limit that may still include differences of visual size but none of visual distance, with all objects having the same visual distance. The camera is merely capable of extending visual space, a fact that can be demonstrated by taking a picture from a height of 3000 meters.

Similarly, one may well perceive the transition of a curvature from the second into the third dimension, but a transition from the third into the fourth dimension can be comprehended neither by our visual sense nor by touch.

Time is only indirectly comprehended by our senses. The change of position of an object in space indicates the passage of time. When the speed of these changes approached the accelerated rate of our modern rhythms, artists thought it necessary to register these phenomena. The Italian futurists have caught the vibrations of quickly moving bodies flitting back and forth in space. However, bodies are brought into motion by means of forces. Suprematism created the dynamic tension of forces. The accomplishment of the futurists and the suprematists is represented by static surfaces characterized by dynamism. These are irrationally transposed and concretized oscillograms of speed and dynamism. Such an approach is quite unsatisfactory. The attempt is to create motion by motion. Boccioni's solution is of a naturalistic character. He connected part of his sculpture to a motor, so that the natural motion of an object was imitated. Tatlin and the constructivists in Moscow have treated motion symbolically. The various parts of the Monument to the Third International revolve around their own axes with relative speeds of one year, one month, one day. In 1921 Prusakov constructed a mobile relief symbolizing, as well as satirizing, in a dadaistic manner the session of a factory committee. Gabo stylized the pendular motion of a metronome (Russian Art Exhibition in Berlin, 1922). The only significant achievements in this direction have been made by modern dynamic advertising, which developed out of the immediate need to affect our psyche, rather than relying on aesthetic reminiscences.

147

We are now at the beginning of a period in which A. is, on the one making hand, degenerating into making pasticci of museum monuments, while, on the other hand, struggling for the creation of a new conception of space. I have demonstrated above that space and objects form a mutually functional relationship. This creates the problem of creating *imaginary* space by means of material objects.

Imaginary Space

Our capacity for visual perception is limited in the apprehension of motion and of the total condition of an object in general: for example, a recurring motion having a frequency of less than $^1/_{30}$ sec. gives the impression of constant motion. The motion picture is based on this principle. The inclusion of motion pictures as a means of realizing tasks of dynamic F. by virtue of actual motion is a definite achievement of V. Eggeling and his successors. It represents the first step in the direction of building up imaginary space. However, the cinema depends on dematerialized surface projection using merely a single facet of our visual faculties. Of course it is well known that a material point in motion is capable of forming a line; for example: a glowing piece of coal in motion gives the impression of a luminous line, while the motion of a material line gives the impression of a surface or a volume. That is only one indication of how elementary solids can be used to construct an object that forms a whole in three-dimensional space while in a state of rest; yet when brought into motion it becomes an entirely new object, i.e., a new space impression that will exist only during the duration of the motion, and is therefore imaginary. (In the original, this chapter was followed by a number of sketches. Ed.)

The infinitely variegated effects that may be achieved by the F. of imaginary space can already be sensed to a limited extent even today. The whole range of all of our visual capacities may thus be brought into play. To name a few: stereoscopic effects of motion by passage through colored media; color impressions produced by superimposition of chromatic clusters of light rays as the result of polarization, etc.; the transformation of acoustic phenomena into visual form. We can safely predict that everyday life will borrow widely from these A. achievements. However, as far as we are concerned, the most important aspect of this development is the fact that this A.-F. will be accompanied by the destruction of the old A. notion of monumentality. Even today the opinion still prevails that A. must be something created for eternity: indestructible, heavy, massive, carved in granite or cast in bronze—the Cheops Pyramid.

The Eiffel Tower is not monumental, for it was not built for eternity but as an attraction for a world fair; no solid masses, but a pierced space needle. We are now producing work which in its overall effect is essentially intangible. For we do not consider a work monumental in the sense that it may last for a year, a century, or a millennium, but rather on the basis of continual expansion of human performance.

In the preceding I have traced the variability of our space conceptions and the subsequent F.'s of A., thus arriving at *nonmaterial materialism*. This sounds like a paradox. However, experience proves that *progress consists of our being compelled to accept and, indeed, to regard as self-evident and essential, views that our forefathers considered incomprehensible and were in fact incapable of comprehending.*

El Lissitzky: Exhibition Rooms*

Task
The organizers of the 1926 International Art Exhibition in Dresden called me from Moscow to design a space for new (constructive) art.

Location and Purpose
Large international art shows resemble a zoo where the visitors are subjected to the roar of thousands of assorted beasts. My space will be designed in such a way that the objects will not assault the visitor all at once. While passing along the picture-studded walls of the conventional art exhibition setup, the viewer is lulled into a numb state of *passivity*. It is our intention to make man *active* by means of design. This is the purpose of space.

Requirements with Reference to the Exhibition Object
The design object of new painting is color: color as an epidermis covering a skeleton. Depending on the construction of the skeleton, the epidermis becomes pure color or tone. Each of these requires a different

---

* Typewritten text in the archives of the Lower Saxony Provincial Museum, Hanover.

illumination and conceptual separation. To achieve an equivalence of effect for all works, an optimum optical environment has to be created for such an exhibition space, similar to optimal acoustic conditions necessary for a concert hall.

Sequential Organization of the Task

(a) One may attempt to create the best background for the painting by using the means of painted as such. Around each work a rectangle of a matching color is painted directly on the wall—and that's all. The wall as a whole confronts the viewer as a painting, for to hang a Leonardo on a wall fresco by Giotto is obviously nonsensical.

(b) I consider the four walls of a given space not as supporting elements or merely as protective planes, but as an optical background for the painting exhibited. Accordingly, I decided to dissolve the wall surface as such.

(c) The space was to accommodate more than one work. Yet, I set myself the goal of avoiding the effect of overcrowding and clutter.

(d) Light, which is the determinant of all color effects, must be controlled.

(e) The space itself must not become some kind of private salon decoration. It should establish a standard for other spaces in which new art is shown to the public.

Sulution to (a) and (b)

I placed thin wood strips (7 cm deep), spaced at intervals of 7 cm, **Fig. 35** against the wall surface. These slats were painted white on the left side and black on the right side, while the wall itself was painted gray. Thus the wall is perceived as white from the left, black from the right, and gray when viewed from the front. Accordingly, and depending on the position of the viewer, the paintings appear against a black, white, or gray background—they have been given a triple life.

Solution to (c)

I further interrupted the system of vertical wood strips by placing a box frame in each corner of the room (5 units, 1.10 to 1.90 meters wide). They were divided in half by a movable surface (a perforated steel plate). Inside, two paintings were placed one above the other behind the sliding plate. While one of the two is fully visible, the other may be partially seen through the perforations of the sliding plate. In this way I have achieved a situation whereby the room accommodates one and a half as many works as a conventional one, while at the same time only half of the works will be seen at any one time.

Solution to (d)

The whole ceiling acts as a light source (stretched unbleached calico). Along the facing wall I introduced blue masking elements and along the opposite wall yellow ones, thus illuminating the one with a *cold* and the other with a *warm* color.

Solution to (e)

By means of such unequivocal design principles I succeeded in realizing a prototype that does not fall into the conventional category of a so-called arts-and-crafts object, but that awaits future standardization.

Effect

When entering the room (entry and exit are indicated by recalling the form of a sculptor's easel) the visitor is faced by a gray wall, a whitish left wall, and a blackish right wall. The varying width of the boxes shifts the visual axes of the space with respect to the center lines of the doors, resulting in a rhythmic expression of the whole. With each motion the visitor makes within the space of the room the effect of the walls changes: i.e., that which was black changes to white and vice versa. Thus an optical dynamic is created as a result of human motion. The game actively involves the viewer. The play of the wall-surface treatment is complemented by the transparency of the cassettes. The viewer is tempted to slide the perforated cover plates up and down, discovering new paintings or covering up those that do not interest him. He is thus physically forced to involve himself with the exhibition objects.

M—Exhibition Booth in the Hanover Museum

The next effort deals with the design of a room housing the collection **Fig. 34** of New Art (from cubism to the present) in the Hanover Museum. Light enters the room through a window that takes up most of the wall. My goal was to transform the window opening into a tectonic element of illumination, designed in such a way as to admit only as much light as required. Near the window I placed two showcases containing four surfaces for watercolor paintings, and so on, all part of a device that allows their rotation about a horizontal axis. One corner, along with a mirror on the wall, was developed for the display of sculpture. A horizontally movable display case (similar to a sliding door) was built into the adjoining wall to hold four larger works; the third wall was designed to accommodate a vertically movable display case for two paintings; and the fourth wall accommodated a display case for three paintings with a pull-blind. Since the light source was from the corner (not from the ceiling as in Dresden), the wall coloring (again white-gray-

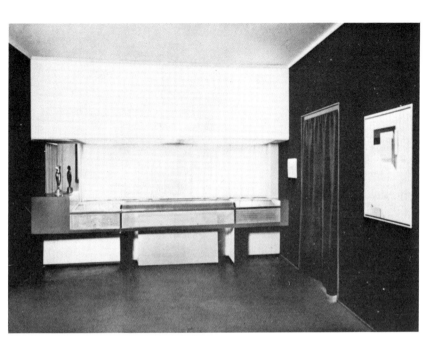

Fig. 34. A window wall in the Cabinet of the Abstractionists. On each side of the heating register were show cases with four viewing surfaces each, which could be manipulated by the visitors. On the right wall a composition by El Lissitzky entitled "Floating Object." Direct light was subdued by cloth wall coverings, and the lower part of the window was shaded by adjustable louvres which could be opened or closed for different light effects.

◀ Fig. 33. El Lissitzky: "Swinging Object," from the Lissitzky folio of the Kestner-Gesellschaft, Hanover.

black) was solved in a different manner. The specifications for the vertical slats called for stainless steel.

M

It was my intention to use periodically changing electric lights to achieve the white-gray-black effect, but unfortunately no electric conduits were available in the new exhibition complex.

Fig. 35. El Lissitzky: Exhibition space with vertical wood slats.

154

III. Reports Concerning Architecture and Urbanism in the USSR, 1928–1933

M. J. Ginsburg, Moscow: Contemporary Architecture in Russia*

The state of modern architecture in Russia, or at least the determining factors influencing its development, can only be comprehended on the basis of an understanding of the living conditions existing in the USSR.

First, I should like to clarify the factors that have impeded the progressive evolution of architecture in that country, with special emphasis on how this has affected actual practice.

Underlying the whole problem is the relatively poor economic situation of the Union, which in turn is the outcome of the difficult and long war and postwar years. Nevertheless, conditions are progressively improving with each passing year. The following table illustrates the present state of affairs in terms of capital investment in the various categories of new construction in the metropolitan areas during the past three years:

Year	1924–5 Million Rubles	1925–6 Million Rubles	1926–7 Million Rubles	1927–8 Million Rubles
Industrial Buildings	370	811	90	1166
Electrification and Related Building Construction	45.2	72.1	151.9	202
Residential and Public Buildings	261		265	456

* From: *Die Baugilde*, Berlin, October 1928, p. 1370–72.

155

In addition, it is important to take into account a large amount of construction activity in a number of smaller cities as well, especially in recent years. This refers to the capitals and main centers of a number of Republics that have agreed to join the Soviet Union. These are Kzyl-Orda, Alma-Ata, Dzhambul in Kazakhstan, Makhach Kala in Dagestan, Frunze in the Kirghiz S. S. R., and Elista in the Kalmuck Territory.

The painfully low level of our technology in general, and of the construction industry in particular, represent a further obstacle to the development of modern architecture in the USSR. In all Western countries, and particularly in America, the extraordinary advances in technology have become the real driving force behind all new movements in architecture. In Russia, however, modern technology and its potential are unfortunately still inadequate for the vast social problems to be solved by modern architecture—problems thrust to the fore by the changed living conditions of the working classes after the October Revolution.

The third obstacle to be overcome by modern architecture in Russia has its counterparts in all other countries as well, namely, the conservatism of the older generation of architects and engineers who received their training before the war in the academies and similar educational institutions. They refuse to recognize the dynamism of contemporary architecture and, in effect, often attempt to thwart its growth. In all fairness, however, it must be said that the number of these reactionaries in the profession has diminished considerably in the past few years. It is therefore not really the fault of the professional opposition if a great number of new buildings do not satisfy present requirements and thus have to be classified as failures; neither can this be rationalized by saying that these designs have miscarried because of the application of antiquated principles. The simple truth is that we have up to now failed to analyze clearly the tasks to be solved and to articulate our goals. Moreover, we have not yet succeeded in finding the appropriate architectural means of expressing these new ideas.

On the other hand, one could list a number of circumstances that are in fact beneficial to new architecture. Its progress—to the extent that we dare use the term—justifies the hope that as the years go by, modern architecture will gradually become acceptable both in theory and practice. These hopes are based on the following assumptions:

1. The rapid growth of our science, especially in the field of technological advances. For example, in comparison to prewar levels, our coal

and crude-oil production has increased 23 percent, while cotton production has increased 12.5 percent. The gross national product, which had decreased considerably during the war and the subsequent civil-war years, has grown rapidly in the last few years. Whereas in the year 1924–25 the gross national product of our national economy was estimated at 55 billion rubles, this figure has risen by 9.5 billion rubles (i.e., 17.5 percent) in the last four years.

Building activity has increased accordingly. During the last three years, approximately 10.5 billion rubles have been invested in new construction, while in 1928 alone 5 billion rubles were spent. This represents an increase of 20 to 25 percent. It must be kept in mind that the bulk of these expenditures represents direct construction costs, excluding expenditures for equipment and furnishings (3.5 billion in 1928 alone).

2. The special character of our social organization and the detailed provisions of our legislation provide great possibilities for modern architecture.

The nonexistence of private land ownership with its accompanying conflict of private interests creates the conditions for unimpeded city and regional planning for densely populated areas, based solely on community welfare and the modification of these plans as the need arises and at any given moment of time, In the same way, state control of the economy in general, and the concentration of all large construction enterprises under central control in particular, allow a planned effort directed at the industrialization of construction, standardization, and the systematic establishment of building standards.

3. One special circumstance that will be particularly significant in furthering the work of modern architects in Russia is the emergence of a new group of clients: the working masses, free of prejudices as far as taste is concerned, and not bound by tradition—factors that have in the past exerted a decisive, dominant influence on the thinking of the petty bourgeoisie. Because of bare economic necessity the millions of workers have no love for the ornamental junk, the holy pictures, and all the thousands of useless articles that usually clutter up middle-class homes. These millions of workers must unquestionably be considered supporters of modern architecture. Their willingness to relinquish certain private desires—which make coherent planning so difficult—should make the transition to constructive building easier and should help to facilitate the industrialization of the building process by means of serial mass production, similar to the process of high-quality mass production in the consumer industries.

157

4. Another fact of the utmost significance is the growing public interest in questions of architecture. The press pays special attention to questions of technology, and problems of modern architecture are also covered extensively in the daily newspapers. Discussions about technical subjects have become a daily occurrence at workers' meetings.

Moreover, surveys are being carried out among the inhabitants of new housing projects, designed to ascertain the true needs of the workers on the one hand, and to teach them to understand the need for simple and rational forms in contemporary architecture on the other.

5. As a consequence of all of this, new architectural teams have formed which have broken unequivocally with academic traditions. Some of these are: ASNOVA (Association of Modern Architects), OSA (Association of Modern Architects—the constructivists), etc. The OSA, for example, has a membership of young architects from ten cities of the USSR united by a common ideal and using similar methods of work. Their common goal is to solve the great architectural tasks posed by the Revolution by means of rational design methods.

6. Modern architecture is gaining more and more influence and validity in the academies, as well as in the intermediate technical institutes. For example, the Moscow institutes, Vkhutein and MVTU, have completely reformed their curriculum during the last few years, and the old methods of teaching architecture have been reduced to an insignificant role in their curricula. Thus, traditional methods of teaching architecture no longer have direct influence on the students' design work. The new curricula vigorously stress a number of entirely new disciplines, such as architectural theory of design, and exercises with space and color.

Thus, we are witnessing the emergence of a generation of young architects who will never be lured back to the eclecticism of the prewar period and who will be charged with the great task of building in a new spirit. The advances of modern architecture are not confined to Moscow alone. From the capital the principles of modern architecture have spread to Leningrad, Kharkov, Kiev, Tomsk, Kazan, Baku, Tiflis, and so on, and there is no doubt that soon there will be no school in the Union that still supports the old tenets of classical eclecticism.

7. In conclusion, it should be pointed out that all construction in the Soviet Union is being regulated by a new system controlled by the state. There is no doubt that the system has made many mistakes and that much has as yet remained untested. Nevertheless, the transition from a privately owned, unregulated construction industry to a planned and centralized

one, committed to rationalization and the reduction of costs, represents an undeniable advance. The Building Committee of the RSFSR is an agency with unlimited powers responsible for the rationalization of the whole building process throughout the whole territory of Russia.

These factors tend to affect Russian architecture in a negative as well as in a positive way and give the existing situation in the USSR its own peculiar flavor. In spite of the fact that until now only a few projects have been realized, each consecutive year can be expected to produce new and important successes. The limited number of modern buildings erected so far should merely be regarded as the first harbingers of the future. Indubitably, the immediate future will produce a number of buildings that will be in full accordance with the new principles of modern architecture. The sum total of the objective facts recited above assures us that contemporary architecture in Russia will gain ground with each passing year.

P. Martell, Berlin: Legislation Concerning Residential Development in the Soviet Union*

The Communist Revolution in Russia, probably the greatest social phenomenon of all time, also created the most unusual conditions in the area of residential development by the planned expropriation of all large private property holdings. In the name of the Communist Revolution, Russian house owners and landholders lost all their property, which became instead the state property of the Communist Soviet Republic. Thus, the Russian state assumed supreme ownership of all buildings, land, and real estate. For practical administrative purposes, all urban real estate was placed under the jurisdiction of the city governments, which were left with the difficult task of making these old, handed-down properties usable by the community. In addition to this, Russian city administrations had to solve another difficult and important problem, namely, the alleviation of prevalent housing shortages by new residential construction. Up to now, new housing has encountered great difficulties, mainly because of shortages of materials, although it should be noted

---

* From: *Wohnungswirtschaft*, XXIII, Berlin 1928, pp. 140–43.

that in a limited number of Russian cities some new residential construction has actually taken place. However, the number of these buildings is so small that it has no real significance in the over-all context of new residential construction in Russia. At present, the technical maintenance of old residential property in the Soviet Union has priority over new residential construction. Due to acute shortage of materials, Russian city administrations are unable to maintain the enormous property holdings handed over to their care in good repair. As a consequence, Russian city dwellings—with only very few exceptions—give the appearance of extensive and frightening decay and dilapidation. In the north of Russia, where buildings are exposed to extreme climatic ravages because of the long and severe winters, decay is even more apparent than in the south. Sewer systems and water-supply lines have been most severely affected, especially in northern cities. There are usually no replacements available for the numerous pipes that have been burst and broken by frost, creating thoroughly disagreeable and unsanitary conditions.

The virtually unlimited expropriation of all private ownership in the Soviet Union was originally based on the general law, promulgating the Basic Rights of the Exploited Working Classes, dated January 13, 1918. To quote: "Private ownership of land and property is to be abrogated; all land holdings are to be declared the property of the whole nation and handed over to the working classes without compensation on the basis of equitable land use. All forests, mineral wealth, and water resources of national importance, all movable as well as immovable inventory, model farm holdings as well as specialized business establishments are to be declared national property." This expropriation law was at first only applied to rural property. The expropriation of urban property was carried out on the basis of numerous other laws. A law of October 20, 1917 prohibited all forms of land speculation. At the same time, all legal procedures concerning the sale or mortgaging of city-owned real estate were declared null and void; offenses against these laws were punished by heavy penalties. In practice, expropriation became complete and universal, since both the municipalities and the local Soviets were granted virtually unlimited powers of disposal over all residential property. Expropriation was placed in the hands of the so-called Commission for Residential Dwellings, which was given arbitrary power of control over all urban real estate. There was, at that time, a predilection for electing former janitors to act as chairmen of these commissions. A Central Commission for Residential Dwellings established in Moscow was granted final executive authority.

As far as expropriation is concerned, Russian Communism has lately willy-nilly recognized the need to reconstitute bourgeois concepts of law to a certain degree. As a result, new real-estate laws have been developed having the following general features as far as urban property laws are concerned: To re-establish a basic legal order for Russian urban policies, the Soviet government has asked all cities to fix their exact municipal boundaries. Such a separation between city and country was considered indispensable, since the law treated urban property somewhat differently from rural property. Thus, the law of December 7, 1925, made it obligatory for all cities to establish their exact municipal boundaries by January 1, 1929. The cities were rather tardy in responding to this request by the Soviet government—by the end of 1926 only 40 percent of all the cities had fixed their municipal boundaries. During the survey carried out for this purpose, a remarkable fact of general cultural significance came to light, namely, that numerous small Russian and Siberian towns did not have any maps or documents on which to base a survey. In other cases, existing city maps were so outdated as to be practically useless. For example, the city plan of the Siberian town of Kainsk, population 10,000, had been drawn up 100 years ago.

The Soviet law of April 13, 1925, regulated urban land policy, insofar as city and municipal administrations were given exclusive jurisdiction over the use and administration of all city land. Thus, Russian city administrations have an almost unlimited and sovereign monopoly of power over laws and regulations concerning all land use within their boundaries. This unrestricted power vested in the city government is limited by only one exception, namely, the use of city land by agencies of the central government operating on the national level, such as railroad stations, military installations, etc. Whenever an agency of the central government is in need of a parcel of city property, a procedural format must first be agreed upon with the respective city administration, and the resulting transaction is subsequently submitted to the Commissariat of the Interior. In each case, the final decision is confirmed in the form of a decree issued by the Council of People's Commissars, which represents the supreme law of the Soviet Union. In all other cases, permits for a dwelling or any other land use within the city limits can be obtained solely from the city administration. Thus, the city represents the highest legal source for the granting of land-use privileges.

Russian cities, especially the bigger ones, soon recognized that even with the best possible organization it was impossible to administer the great multitude of all their buildings through one single central agency. Even though some municipalities made an attempt to run all their properties from City Hall, most of the other cities preferred to forgo such a method. These cities decided to place individual buildings in the care of and for the use of individual citizens, or public or private corporations. In each case the caretakership was put under contract, which in turn gave the user certain litigable rights.

The Communist Soviet Union has recently introduced two kinds of land rent: the so-called base rent, and the differential or supplementary rent. The Russian law of November 12, 1925, provided the legal basis for rental duties concerning urban real estate and land used for transportation purposes. The "basic rent" represents a duty payment due to the state as the sole and supreme owner of all land. It is levied on each house or property within the city limit and is uniform for all parts of the city. One is struck by the use of the term "uniform" in the provision, which ignores the position of property with respect to transportation, so that each house, regardless of its relative location, is assessed equally. Obviously, such a system of rents is inequitable and unjust. The level of the prime rent to be paid to the state is computed on the basis of the approximate average annual yield attained by the agricultural enterprises surrounding the city. Consequently, there is no uniform basic rent, and each Russian Republic pays the national government a differently apportioned contribution. Since the level of the basic rent is tied to the economic viability of the surrounding farms, it is obvious that compared to smaller cities the metropolitan areas have to pay a higher basic rent not only because of their larger over-all area but also because they provide a big market for the surrounding farm country, thus guaranteeing a higher agricultural turnover with correspondingly higher profits. It is evident that such a system of assessment is built on extremely shaky foundations.

The other Russian Communist land rent is the so-called differential rent which in contrast to the national basic rent represents a supplementary rent payable to the city. This supplementary rent which has to be paid to the city by the owner of a house or by the holder of property for its use is differentiated depending on the size and the location of the property. National property and municipal property used for direct city services are exempt from any rent. For the establishment and the levying of due basic and differential rents, the Soviet Union has appointed special assessment commissions that are supposed to operate on a completely impartial basis. A Central Assessment

Commission, acting as the highest authority for the whole Soviet Union, has been formed. Since the Soviet Union consists of many individual republics—the Ukraine being but one example—each of these Republics has its own state assessment commission along with a number of subordinate regional assessment commissions. A further organizational breakdown leads to the various district assessment commissions which deal with assessments of basic and differential rents of towns belonging to their own district. Decisions made by the district assessment commissions may be appealed to the regional assessment commission. In practical terms, both of the land rents described above have not had any great impact on state income, since they have fallen far short of their estimated goals. Against an estimated annual total income of 9 million gold rubles of revenues from basic rents alone, only 3 million gold rubles were actually collected.

The Soviet law of May 29, 1924, made an attempt to establish a new rate scale for the basic rents, but it soon became apparent that these rates were too high, for in many cases the estimates were higher than the income received from the leases. In the meantime the government has attempted by means of numerous decrees to create more economically tolerable conditions in the individual cities by lowering the rates. To give an insight into the urban land policies of the Soviet Union we present several items from the report of the People's Commissariat of the Interior. The official census deals with 251 of the 539 cities of the Russian Soviet Socialist Republics. In it, land within city limits is classified according to four categories: 1. Land directly administered by central government agencies, comprising approximately 4.4 percent of the total urban land area. 2. Land used for dwelling and construction, i.e., the actual residential areas of the cities, covering approximately 12.6 percent of the total area. 3. Public land used for traffic, recreation and play areas, cemeteries, and garbage dumps. This category also includes rivers and lakes. These public open areas use up 12.4 percent of the total area of the city. Since a great number of Russian cities are still without water and sewerage systems, these are often replaced by cesspools and garbage dumps. Areas used for such purposes are very often quite large in certain cities, often as much as 2 percent of the total. 4. The so-called "useful appurtenances," covering the remaining 70.6 percent of the total land area. These include grazing lands, farm land, meadows, vegetable gardens, and fruit gardens. It should be noted that in the first few years after the Revolution the cities failed to engage in land cultivation altogether, resulting in extreme neglect and deterioration of these areas. Only lately has land cultivation been resumed, though on a very modest scale. To some extent the high rents charged by the cities for the use of such land were responsible for this neglect. In 1925, for example, the average rent for a hectare of vegetable garden was 62 marks, and for agricultural land, 14 marks. Thus, large areas of urban open land lay fallow.

In spite of all this, certain planning policies are being gradually evolved by the Soviet cities. Quite obviously, Russian city administrations show great interest in questions dealing with all aspects of new construction. However, absolutely no means were available for new construction, since during the first years of the existence of the Soviet Republic, development on the whole became bogged down in the theoretical planning stage, a trend which in general tends to permeate much of political life in the USSR. The city administration, acting as the sole representative of supreme state land ownership, is the only agency authorized to acquire land parcels for new construction, and at the same time also controls all new construction. The widespread shortage of residential accommodations in Russian cities is the direct result of the inadequate living conditions prevailing in rural areas, which in turn results in part of the rural population leaving the villages in the hope of finding shelter and refuge in the cities. Although leading officials in the top echelons of the Soviet government are fully conversant with the theories and ideas of modern city planning, this is not all the case with many city administrations. The government tries to correct this situation by sending out numerous circulars expounding the principles of modern city planning, but so far only modest success has been achieved. In 1922, the People's Commissariat of the Interior founded a central archive in Moscow with the dual purpose of collecting and classifying the plans of all Russian cities. Both in Moscow and Leningrad museums were founded dealing exclusively with municipal and communal affairs. An Academy of Communal Affairs was established in Leningrad in 1923 with a similar purpose. There is no shortagh of architectural city-planning competitions. Eventually, however, all these proposals pass into oblivion, since the means for their realization are lacking. The general level of impoverishment in Russia at this time prevents any kind of high-level resolve in terms of practical implementation.

As in other matters, the Soviet Union had to make a decision concerning the creation of a new construction law. The first revolutionary law dealing with this matter was issued on August 8, 1921, but soon after was superseded by the Construction Law of August 14, 1922, which established certain fundamental concepts. Although this law was later amended a number of times—as, for example, by the law of November 21, 1927—it nevertheless fixed procedures for building-law contracts. On the basis of the latter, a developer may acquire from the city administration the right to use a specific empty or built-on property; in the case of masonry construction, the contract is valid for 65 years, and in the case of wood construction, for 50 years. In return, the developer assumes the obligation to actually erect a building on the lot. In order to encourage private individuals to build, the Soviet building laws have gradually extended use rights on properties from an initial 40 years to a possible 65-year period. After expiration of the use right, the building becomes the property of the city. In this connection it should be mentioned that the USSR has in principle abolished all rights of inheritance. Nevertheless, during the life of the 65-year use-right period, property may be transferred to an heir. One is also permitted to sell or to mortgage the right to build. The right-to-build contract is granted upon payment of a definite lease rental to the city. Insofar as construction of residential buildings with a minimum of 75 percent of the floor area devoted to dwellings is concerned, certain ameliorations are granted. The 65-year use right represents a very long time span, and one cannot escape the impression that in this case we are really dealing with a quasi "property right," in spite of the fact that the teachings of Communism categorically deny and reject all notions of private property.

Special attention should further be paid to the fact that after the expiration of the 65-year use right, masonry structures do not automatically become the free property of the city, but appropriate compensation must be paid by the city to the holder of the use right. This fact reveals a surprising recognition of the concept of the right to private property. The law of December 21, 1926, goes even further in the case of residential building cooperatives by granting them perpetual land-use rights. Even previous building contracts of such cooperatives have been modified, and the cooperatives were retroactively granted the right of perpetual use. In addition, explicit property rights have been granted to the Soviet Building Cooperatives, assuring them of full legal protection for all dwellings erected by them. Thus, in spite of its frequent official rejection of the whole concept the Soviet government has clearly and unequivocally recognized the right to private property as far as this particular case is concerned. Since Russia does not possess enough of its own financial resources to embark upon extensive building activities, the Soviets have tried to attract foreign construction firms. Except for a few exceptions, such firms have been reluctant to participate. As far as Germany is concerned, only the firm Paul Kossel of Bremen has declared its willingness to engage in major construction activities in Russia, late in 1926. This work is being done in cooperation with the Russian Central Association of Residential Building Cooperatives and is funded by a newly formed stockholding company—the Russgerstroi. Residential buildings made of concrete are the main concern of this company.

In conclusion it may be said that in Russia too, residential construction has advanced somewhat during the last few years, even though progress has been rather modest. Ultimately all residential building is really a question of capital, and this has quite naturally proven an especially difficult obstacle in impoverished Russia.

Bruno Taut: Russia's Architectural Situation*

All thoughts in Russia are dominated by industrialization and the concurrent opening up of its vast virgin territories, rich in natural resources but lacking the technical equipment for their exploitation. Architectural thought is directed toward the same goals. Industrial building and the industrialization of building are foremost among the concerns of Russian architects who have come to the West to study, to visit, and to collect information; they also feature prominently in the questions Russians ask when speaking to Western architects visiting Russia. Russian industrial buildings are conceived in the same consistent, functional manner as are ours here in the West: in Holland, in France, partially in England, and above all in America. The Ford plant in Detroit could just as well have been built in Russia, with minor modifications necessitated by different climatic conditions, and the new plant by Ford in Nizhnii-Novgorod will indeed soon confirm this contention. The architectural problem as such in the field of industrial building has ceased to exist, since the definition of purpose is unequivocal and, in terms of its goals, can just about be determined with mathematical precision, so that it is possible today to speak about a virtually universal reflex of appropriate architectural design habits. Indeed, one is tempted to say that the difficulties that have surrounded this problem have been overcome.

Even though the USSR is totally committed to the economic exploitation of its territories, especially under the influence of the five-year plans, there are indications that there are areas of productive work that are not immediately affected by this tendency and that cannot subsist by virtue of a purely scientific point of view, even though the economy has been raised to the level of state planning, thus injecting elements of a moral and ethical nature into the situation. This much is evident: when individual self-interest is superseded by work for the community, new sources of ideas, as well as new spiritual resources, have to be tapped to provide this higher usefulness with continuing purpose.

In the publication *New Russia* (Vol. 5/6, 1929) the Greek poet Nikolai Kazan writes in his "Banquet of Georgian Poets" about an important conversation with the Georgian poet Robakidze, who is quoted as having said the following: "It is the purpose of art to express the invisible breath of the father in a tactile and visible manner. If man

---

* Apparently an unpublished manuscript. Berlin, November 2, 1929.

does not succeed beyond merely expressing or describing the son, then his art must be considered superficial and insignificant . . .''; and further on: "The Russian Revolution is a visible phenomenon of a larger cosmic revolution that is being prepared in our hearts. The poet must come to understand the deep meaning of Bolshevism; he is its son, and only through it can he search and find the father . . . .''—And Meyerhold, whose theater was the precursor of purism, of mechanized "objectivity" and the abstraction of acting, has recently confessed that ". . . beauty must now come to the stage. We must inundate the theater with beauty!'' Surely there is no danger that Meyerhold will conjure up an arts-and-crafts stage in the manner of Max Reinhardt of 30 years ago. Nevertheless, by means of objectivity on the one hand and by abstraction on the other, art strives to capture all the human senses by illuminating the universal by means of concrete reality.

The absence of such a harmonious point of view, which possibly only the Mexican Diego Rivera has brought to realization in painting, may well have been what prevented Lenin in his time from becoming the friend of revolutionary artists, apart from the fact that he may not have considered the arts of great importance in general; at any rate, even the durable People's Commissar, Lunacharski, was unable to give these trends full priority. As a result, we have the well publicized debate in the Soviet press—initiated by Gorki—and reported in our press as well, which discussed the merits and value of a thorough study of classical literature.

Architecture cannot ignore these spitirual currents; on the contrary, it is fully part of them, particularly if it is to transcend the trite concerns of a purely functional approach. Basically, there is no limit to such an approach; but, as mentioned before, the design of straightforward industrial buildings does not recognize this problem at all, or only partially, since, strictly speaking, the problem as such is in fact the result of pure functional necessity. It was quite proper to reduce architecture to its basic functional aspects, thus ending the confusion of mixing or confounding it with painting and sculpture, and so at long last destroying its image as one of the decorative arts. Even though the Russians, and we as well, have thrown off this particular yoke, a new tendency has to be fought these days, namely, the tendency to proclaim that functionalism and objectivity are the highest aims of architecture. Functionalism in the sense of trite utilitarianism or, even worse, mere consideration of cost and profit, would surely mean the death of architecture. The dissipation of the achievements of the pioneers of modern

168

architecture shows very clearly how much damage can be done if such a thesis is accepted. Function, understood in the sense that the whole building as well as all its component parts, its spaces, and ultimately even its exterior are permeated by a consistent spirit, will give architecture a new lease on life and re-establish it as an art in the aesthetic sense as well. This is borne out by the fact that a number of existing examples already manifest the first ingredients of such new beauty. A similar case can be made about the question of objectivity. In a positive sense the consequences are the same as described above. In the negative sense the results may turn out to be even worse: instead of seeing his task as one of building, the architect sees it as one of making programs for building. Whereas in the past he did not concern himself at all, or only very little, with the needs and wants that led to building, he now attempts to deal with these questions all by himself. A drastic example of this is the workingman's dwelling, which the architect wants to reform according to his own ideas, and which is usually designed for the "new" dweller, who is made to fit the preconceived notion of the architect in question. Our own situation is full of examples that prove that such experiments, should they become the rule, inevitably lead to an even more extensive proletarianization of the working classes than before. In order to arrive at a true understanding of the whole situation, a knowledge of the worker's life, and poverty in general, is necessary to provide food for one's imagination. Seen in this light, many of the exhibited plans and model layouts take on the semblance of a charity tea "for the benefit of the poor."

In Russia these, as it were, self-induced dilemmas of modern architecture are quite naturally expressed in a different manner. However, as soon as residential construction there overcomes its primitive form of organization, which so far has prevented it from arriving at any kind of concrete achievement, the same dilemmas as those described above will have to be faced. Still, the Russians sense this danger, and it is quite possible that they are resisting modern architecture on the basis of their observations of developments abroad—often *in toto*—simply because they do not understand the exact nature of the danger. Such an opposition, devoid of any real argument, and which because of a revolutionary ideology feels that it is being pushed toward a moral schism according to the laws of polarity, is now faced by architect-artists whose *a priori* worship of modern architecture, of construction, materials, concrete, steel, glass, etc., is essentially as unjustified as the position of their opponents.

These moderns want to imbue the "new" materials with revolutionary ideology, thus elevating them to symbols of their age. Furthermore, it is really very difficult for an outsider to understand the difference between the so-called "constructivists" and the "formalists." Often, these new designs are accompanied by tables of statistical or quasiscientific character, and the Scheerbart "lucky numbers" are greeted with ecstatic delight. Another import from the West: German city plans and/or building projects, covered with minute descriptions, the whole sheathed in scientific lingo, certainly may be partially blamed for all this confusion.

It appears that the inhibitions of both parties have the same basic source. On the one hand ideology, science, materials; on the other, force, monumentality, representation, with both attempting to quench the thirst for beauty, However, the real sources seem as mysterious as ever.

America teaches us a good lesson concerning European weaknesses, insofar as it mirrors them as caricatures in their ultimate distortion. I received a publication notice from New York, advertising a new book with the title *The Logic of Modern Architecture*. I awaited its delivery impatiently. Now that the book has arrived, I ask myself what it really tells me about American architectural logic. For example, the façade of a theater is considered logical if "dramatic," that of a movie theater, if "theatric"—which leaves us with absolutely no doubt that both must be pure corn. Stone ornaments are proclaimed to be logical if they appear to be sharp and metal-like, thus "harmonizing" with the metal frames of the doors and windows of the storefront of a skyscraper. Even without looking at the illustrations it is evident that we have here another set of prerequisites for nothing but pure tripe. The ideas generally disseminated in Europe about "logic" in architecture are essentially just as inane. Here too the demands for representativeness and monumentality occupy first place, and nations are quick to agree when distortions of architectural conceptions are concerned (cf. the Palace of Nations in Geneva, the San Domingo Light House, etc.), and of course in Germany it has become an unchangeable dictum that a church must represent piety. This tends to obscure the boundaries between faddish movie sets and real buildings completely and dissipates the strength of modern architecture in the direction of fuzziness or pseudoscience. Both are equally dangerous insofar as the new concepts of architecture have not yet been universally accepted—at least by leading architects—and may eventually impede the evolution of architecture as such.

In Russia the search for fundamentals takes on dramatic forms. There, as anywhere else, human weakness become part of the struggle as manifested in competiton work and its results, where over and over again we can see the conflict between design for a functional purpose as opposed to the quest for beauty. In a limited competition for the projected building of the Great Lenin Library on a prominent site in Moscow, the brothers Vesnin unquestionably submitted the best plans. However, rightly or wrongly, it was found that their modern façade was not the logical solution to the problem because of its large glass areas. And so it was apparently decided to give the commission to an academician who responded more positively to the craving for monumentality with corresponding sacrifices of functional clarity in the layout. In accord with the above-mentioned American "logic," a case like this does call for monumentality, thereby helping this kind of logic to victory, simply because the weak spot of the counter argument was easy to spot, in spite of the fact that there was no question about its advantages in terms of all its other qualities. Another such situation exists with respect to another building in a large governmental complex near the Kremlin. Le Corbusier's design for the building of the Centrosoyus illustrates a similar process, albeit with a different set of characteristics: in place of monumentality we are here dealing with pseudorational artistry presented by a brilliant talent, far beyond the comprehension of Moscow.

A number of functional and important buildings point the way in the direction of future developments, even in Russia. Among these are the buildings of the Electrical Technical Institute, the Textile and Aerohydrodynamic Institute, the Stadium, the Institute of Mineralogy by Vesnin, the Moscow Planetarium and, to a certain degree, the Kharkov Administration Building. In time the present overriding tendency to express the heroism of the Revolution in monuments and buildings will hopefully be overcome. The provisional Mausoleum of Lenin, which is currently being replaced by a permanent structure, has in general been treated in a restrained manner, the exception being the small Greek temple at its top, which illustrates the common error of mistaking architecture for literature. The Lenin Institute, completed in 1925, is another example of a building designed to express "dignity" and "strength" by its great black bulk of stone. The extent to which its real architectural performance has suffered may be gauged by the gloomy and extremely heavy appearance of the building, especially

171

with respect to the striking contrast this produces within the charming cityscape of Moscow to its immediate vicinity. One may also note the complete inability to provide a good solution for the urbanistically very important Place of the Soviets, which now will be very difficult to save. The gloomy and ponderous character of this effort represents the hallmark of a period for a whole school of architects who designed not only office buildings but also apartment houses and clubs in this particular manner. Still, these are not half as bad as the horrible academic misconceptions of the Main Telegraph Office, in which both plan and façades are equally hopeless. As far as the Lenin Institute and its companions are concerned, one can see these as the first ponderous attempts of the Russian *muzhik* trying his first steps in a new direction.

The task of Russian architecture can be seen as an attempt to bring these new ideas into harmony with the traditional Russian closeness to the soil. In Russia this is no empty phrase, but a fact; for in their colors, dances, music, and folk-art the Russians reveal in a visible and tactile manner a true national tradition. Therefore the transformation of something modern into something heavy and cumbersome merely means that a synthesis has not yet been achieved; but is also means that a start has nevertheless been made. Indeed, if one has some feeling for such imponderables, one can sense that this process is at work even now as far as the above-mentioned buildings are concerned. Just as the Russians accept as natural the idea of a fusion of opposites in their philosophy, so they may possibly also succeed in eventually translating the fusion of apparent contradictions into concrete reality. The artists among the architects are not being taken seriously as such by practicing professionals and engineers. However, when obliged to work together with the latter group, the artistry of the atelier changes under the influence of the practicians into heavy, earthbound construction and form, and, in spite of some vague references to Western ideas, the results eventually wind up having typically Russian traits. This is best exemplified by the new stadium. Even though the overriding influence of the engineer is quite evident in its design, its peculiar ponderous quality really belongs to the sphere of the Russian conception of art.

"The artist, whose efforts are directed toward style as against the realization of the organic and natural, and who is looked upon even by his contemporaries as a stylemaker will never reach the shores of the next generation, but will be drowned by the first impending wave of a new tendency." This truth was spoken by Wilhelm von Scholz in *Hier schreibt Berlin*, (*Here Writes Berlin*) and will probably eventually prove true for Russia as well. After all, things are not moving very fast in other places either. Even in our country a lot of work passes under the label of "modern architecture," when in fact it represents nothing so much as some kind of poster publicity designed to announce itself to the world and proclaim something of a basically literary nature, which includes among other notions the much bandied about slogan of "Neue Zeit." Genuine efforts in this direction are difficult to put into words, for their essence seems to be withdrawn from the great general brouhaha; which means that at the present it is hard to imagine how a new school could be founded under such conditions. The quality worth striving for could be compared to ultraviolet rays for which there is no human perceptual sense organism—not yet, at any rate. Perhaps such a sense organism will develop in the course of future generations. Perhaps it will then no longer be necessary to speak about architecture in literary terms; perhaps it will no longer be necessary to speak about architecture at all, because it will then exist as a natural living phenomenon.

City Councillor May's Russian Plans*

A Gigantic Building Task

During a recent interview, Frankfurt City Councillor May made some interesting remarks concerning his immediate plans in Russia. He will be leaving the city on September 1, to take charge of a gigantic Russian building program to be carried out under his direction.

In recent years the Soviet Union has invited many noted scholars from abroad to give lectures on important topics of current interest, among them Councillor May, who spoke at the University of Moscow and also at the University of Leningrad on the subjects of "The New City," "The State of Residential Building in Germany," and "The Rationalization of Residential Construction." The Russian government asked him to give an additional lecture to a small group of important specialists on the theme: "Organizational Proposals Concerning Russian City Planning and Residential Policies."

* From: *Bauwelt*, XXXVI, Berlin 1930, p. 1156.

After some extensive studies of Russian conditions, May acquiesced. A translated version of his proposals was published in all Russian newspapers. The proposals of this German architect made a great impression, and the government invited him to go ahead and set up the whole organization *with a staff of German assistants.* With the active help of the Foreign Office and the German Embassy in Moscow this contract has now been ratified. Thus, twenty-one German gentlemen, with May as their leader, will travel to Moscow on September 1.

City Building—City Expansion

"I am fully aware of the magnitude of my task, and also of the fact that nothing like it has ever been attempted before," Ernst May said recently. "People who know Russia may be surprised that these plans involving billions have been entrusted to a German. American influence in the Soviet Republics is presently very extensive, and thus there were great expectations in the USA that Americans would be given the opportunity to tackle this problem too. The explanation of what happened in this case is that the American skyscraper approach has been more or less rejected by the Russians. They do not wish to hear any more about it. But new cities will have to be built, and old ones will have to be rebuilt. Streets and roads are needed because the sites on which these cities will eventually rise are now desolate steppes. This is the task which has been entrusted to me, to be realized within the over-all framework of the Five-Year Plan, and for which I obviously will be able to lay the foundation only. Something like fifty years will probably be needed for full completion. I am not interested in politics. I am a German architect fulfilling a contract with the Russian government in the hope of helping the German economy a little at the same time. And now concerning my work. First, the most interesting but also the most difficult task: *the creation of entirely new cities*, the first large-scale attempt to realize this much talked-about innovation. The importance of the individual family will be reduced; families will live in small residential cubicles to be considered as bedrooms only. Instead, we shall provide large communal kitchens, kindergartens, clubs, lecture halls, reading halls, sport facilities, etc. All this has already been tested in various situations on a smaller scale, but now for the first time a whole series of new cities will be created out of nothing. If we take a cross-section through a typical apartment building, we find, for instance, that the same things happen in all the kitchens during certain hours of the day. Housewives hover over their stoves cooking. According to Russian theories, this is a waste of time. The situation can be simplified and improved by centralization and rationalization. These cities will primarily be the centers of iron and steel industries, which are to be newly created.

Another task is city expansion. In this respect, Moscow must be considered first. Presently, the city has a capacity for accommodating 800,000 people but is actually populated by 2,000,000. In certain areas of the capital, conditions are truly catastrophic. In addition to planning new cities and expending old ones, I will also head an institution for Russian students in city planning. To date, fifty candidates, selected by the Russian government, have already enrolled."

Ernst May: From Frankfurt to the New Russia*

We here publish Ernst May's first report of his impressions of the Soviet Union and of his work there. May, who has taken over the supervision of the Russian building program will be reporting regularly to our readers about his new activities.   [The Editors]

We started our work five weeks ago, while at the same time striving to familiarize ourselves with, and accustom ourselves to, the conditions of our new country, in spite of our inadequate knowledge of the language. We scattered in all directions to collect the required material. Some pitched their tents in the observatory, drawing on the existing wealth of scientific data to obtain a graphic record of the climatic conditions of the country, always noting the corresponding Frankfurt figures as a basis for comparison. Others turned to diligent studies of their flora, especially in the well kept botanical gardens in Moscow; theirs will be the task of designing the green areas in our plans. If the plan should ask for it, they will conjure up landscaped spaces in the barren steppe. We were given numerous lectures, designed to familiarize us with the basic architectural principles of Russian residential building as well as of hospital and school construction. Members of the Building Research Institute (a counterpart of our own Research Institute for the Management of Building and Residential

---

* From: *Frankfurter Zeitung*, No. 892, November 30, 1930.

Development) showed us in a highly interesting building exhibition that Russia has already done some very extensive and valuable work in this field. During inspection tours of new buildings in the capital, we became aware of those areas in which the earnest striving of the country for a creative realization of the new spirit that permeates all of life here has been crowned by success, as well as of those areas in which additional efforts will be required to make up deficiencies.

Then, suddenly and without advance notice, we received a call informing us of our immediate departure for Magnitogorsk, located in the Kirghiz Steppe, not far from the eastern foothills of the Ural Mountains. A staff of assistants was assembled, and within 24 hours the 5000-km round trip was underway on board a special coach. The journey was anything but a hardship. Jokingly we remembered our Frankfurt cautioners who had predicted, and at times wished on us, death by starvation in the Russian steppe. They should have seen the crates of caviar, chocolate, cigarettes, sausages, and many other goods supplied to us during the trip, and (since I can already hear the scornful mocking of our skeptics) I must also mention the peasant women who offered us eggs, milk, butter, and poultry at almost every train stop. As soon as our train would come to a halt for a longer time (and this happened quite often!) our Jelenichka would hurry to the hot-water kettle of the station to fetch water for our tea. Thus, we often had fresh tea seven or eight times a day while taking turns at preparing our own meals in our cozy compartments with the help of our many-talented interpreter. From the very first day until the end of the trip we were overcome by that special kind of good humor that often fills the long hours of a wait in a dugout or the long evenings in an alpine ski hut. For example, it is impossible to describe our joy and satisfaction on such occasions when our Jelenichka filled her mouth with water from a cup and then—like an elephant in a zoo—sprayed the floor of our compartment for better sweeping, using her mouth as a high-pressure nozzle; or when, at one of the stations, she climbed down from the high train platform to pick up some mysterious stuff lying between the rails to be used for washing our dishes. During such situations, and on certain other occasions, our thoughts inevitably turned to our dear Frankfurt health official and his good advice.

The journey lasted four and a half days (which is considered short by Russian standards), and still time passed quickly. The landscape is of immense breadth, but never boring. For an instant our view was enlivened by deep ravines carved into the clay soil by rain, while a moment later we were passing through swamps with jungle-like underbrush, and immediately after we found ourselves crossing wild streams with shorelines that had their own peculiar charm. The villages seemed to grow out of the very soil. The wooden walls of the huts were brown, while the roofs were covered with yellow-brown straw or wood. In some cases they were dominated by orthodox churches, in others, in parts settled by the Moslem population, they huddled beneath mosques with minarets. As a rule the villages seemed bare, without any kind of tree growth worth mentioning, and only later did we notice settlements that looked more like spacious garden cities. While passing through a district settled by Volga Germans, we learned that we were looking at typical rural block houses, each different from the other but all bearing witness to the German origin of their inhabitants. Fruit and ornamental bushes had been lovingly planted, and whole villages were quite often surrounded by a continuous fence. Later, we entered the Bashkir Republic. At the stops we studied the faces of the people pressing against the train and tried to guess their racial origin. On the evening of the third day we began crossing the Ural Mountains. Bare peaks similar to those of the Rhön Mountains gradually gave way to a most charming low alpine landscape. During a dark night in Zlatoust we saw the glitter of innumerable lights in the workers' settlements near the armament factories creeping up the hillsides along their broad fronts. For a few rubles I bought a charming stone collection that graphically demonstrated the varied and rich mineral wealth still buried below the Ural Mountains. In Khrebet we traversed a mountain pass that connects Europe to Asia. The next morning we arrived in Chelyabinsk, the capital of the Ural Region, and later continued south, along a branch line, leaving behind the main line going to Omsk. We could immediately see by the faces of the native population that here was a different ethnic group. Their slanted eyes revealed that we were now dealing with Mongols. We had arrived in the land of the Kirghizes. The train traversed a steppe covered with hoarfrost. We did not see many villages, but flocks of horses of all colors roamed freely across the frozen soil.

We slowly approached our destination on a temporary rail spur. Fog gave way to clear skies, and our eyes beheld a fascinating spectacle. From the middle of the steppe arose a number of flat hills and among these, one of larger size—a mountain of iron ore. One hundred and fifty million tons of rich iron-ore deposits are located in this area, ready to be surface-mined. In order to exploit these deposits, the second largest industrial complex in the world has been planned here as part of the great Soviet program of industrialization. Coal for smelting the ore will be brought from Kuznetsk, located near the north slopes of the Altai Mountains nearly 2000 kilometers away; on the return journey, the iron will be transported back to Kuznetsk for refining. In addition to the actual smelting and iron works, the industrial complex of Magnitogorsk will include a chemical plant that will utilize the by-products of coke production for aniline-dye refining. A dam, collecting the waters of the Ural River into a reservoir extending 14 square kilometers, to supply the complex with water, offers eloquent testimony to the magnitude of this project. As far as the industrial component of the complex is concerned, 40 percent of the first phase has so far been completed. Generally speaking, the work pace in Russia is somewhat more leisurely than that in Western Europe. This impelled me to put a sign reading *protiv zavtra* (not tomorrow) on the door of my Moscow office. *Zavtra* is the standard answer to all requests to carry out a task somewhat more quickly than usual. Well, in Magnitogorsk this slogan has become superfluous, for work is being pushed ahead with feverish speed under the supervision of Special Government Commissar Schmidt. The one-kilometer-long concrete dam designed to hold back the waters of the Ural River was poured in 75 days, and the electric power station that will be the second largest of its kind after that of Dniepropetrovsk is being erected in three uninterrupted work shifts, even during the winter months. Only a few years ago horses grazed in this part of the steppe, and every so often a small cart drawn by a horse would clatter along the well-worn wagon trails. Now 40,000 workers, living in temporary barracks, apply their labor to one of the mightiest industrial ventures of our time. The innumerable blinking lights of the labor camp and the bright floodlights used for night work made an unforgettable impression on our minds.

Immediately after our arrival we drove in Ford cars to the American sector of the camp, a distance of 4 kilometers from the railroad station. This clean, small barracks settlement was placed right against the slopes of the iron-ore mountain. During our four-day stay there we were excellently provisioned. We commenced work immediately, for there was no need to waste time. We spent many hours exploring the steppe, looking out for topographical irregularities that would affect the planning of a city for 120,000 inhabitants. The view toward the long range of the Ural peaks was of incomparable beauty.

The most important building in the life of Magnitogorsk was a rough brick structure—the administration. It housed the offices of the consultants of the American firm entrusted with the construction of the industrial plant, all of them energetic and clearheaded individuals. Here, we also met some German engineers who were consulting on the construction of the silicate plant. People seem to come and go in droves. All the supervisors had cars at the ready, rushing them to the widely separated parts of the various projects under construction. Everywhere we went, we were given every possible support, both from the Russian officials and the Americans, which enabled us to collect all the relevant material in a mere four days, allowing us in turn to get on with our work on the basis of carefully selected data. We transformed one of our train compartments into a drafting room and during the four-day return journey managed to produce the first drafts of our proposal, using the charcoal supplied as fuel for the samovar as pencils and drafting boards made of plywood pieces as a drawing base. In another compartment the reports were being typed.

The tempo in our Moscow offices is even more hectic than that in Magnitogorsk, for it is necessary to complete this comprehensive task by the end of the month. While all of us are intensely aware of being witnesses to history in the making, we are even more grateful for the privilege of being able to contribute to this great effort within the limits of our humble talents.

M. Ilyin, Moscow: Russian Urbanism*

In connection with industrial recovery in the USSR, problems of urbanism have been vigorously debated in Russia during the last two years. Two diametrically opposed theories have evolved so far, and both have been widely discussed in print. Sabsovich, the author of one of these theories, demands that all newly founded cities belong to an urban type having all the characteristics of a Socialist community, based on a completely communal way of life and the accompanying dissolution of the family. Such "urbanism" desires to create industrial towns as well as agricultural towns with fixed populations (ca. 50,000), providing collective housing for all the inhabitants. This theory is opposed by the "constructivists," under the leadership of the architects Ginsburg and Okhitovich who are proposing so-called "linear cities." This group of

* From: *Wasmuths Monatshefte für Baukunst und Städtebau*, V, Berlin 1931, pp. 237–40.

architects considers the contrast between city and country to be one of the principal mistakes of the capitalist system, and they wish to bridge this gap by advancing a theory that, in effect, proposes complete de-urbanization and an amalgamation of all real and formal boundaries between city and country. All cities are to be dissolved, meaning that even Moscow would be reduced to a park with a few representative buildings remaining. Residential development would no longer be allowed to develop in a radial fashion around industry, but would be planned in a predetermined, regular way, i.e., in long strips along traffic arteries which in turn would relate intimately to life-sustaining agricultural production. In this type of scheme, each individual would be supplied with his own industrially produced small house. Such residential development obviously presupposes extensive development of all types of traffic and transport facilities; but aside from this it has other serious defects. For example, there is a complete separation of dwelling, administration, and work centers, while frequent intersections of residential strips would eventually be hard to avoid. In the end this may well result in an unplanned city of the conventional type.

The material that has come out of the violent discussions concerning these two theories is now incorporated into plans slated for actual implementation. At the moment 38 new cities are being developed in Russia alone.

One of the most interesting and most radical development plans is that of the Socialist city of Novosibirsk, being built on the left bank of the Ob opposite the old city. The new Novosibirsk has been growing at a speed that can only be compared to the rapid pace of American city growth. It is being developed into the most important urban center in Siberia. Its spacious layout is the work of the architects Babenkov, Vlassov, and Poliakov. The construction of the huge industrial complex for the manufacture of "combines" is the most important element of the plan and vitally affects the general planning concept of the new city. All matters concerning the relationship between dwelling and work are being taken into consideration in advance by the planners. The new city is situated between two main railroad lines on a high plateau that falls off steeply toward the river Ob. The industrial district is separated from the industrial district by means of a 750–meter wide green belt. The location of industry in the north of the city is determined by taking into account the prevailing winds from the southeast. In the city itself, rows of so-called "communal houses" are separated by green belts

500 to 650 meters wide. The dwellings cover 15 to 20 percent of the strips dedicated to residential land use; the remaining area of the city is reserved for parks and gardens. The linear dwelling areas consist of "communal housing," proletarian dwellings for 800 to 1000 people, and regular four-story apartment blocks. Each so-called "communal house" has attached to it a nursery, a kindergarten, a dining hall, clubs, and sports facilities. All these service structures are two stories high. The buildings are oriented north to south along their long axis, without regard to important street directions, so as not to coincide with the prevailing wind direction. Three large boulevards are designed to

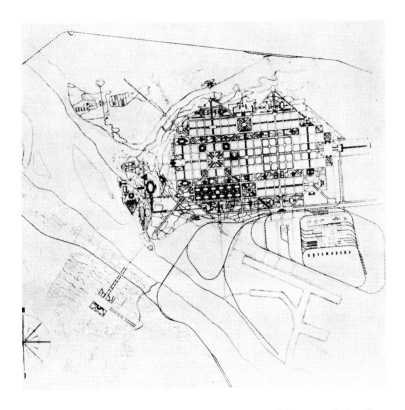

Fig. 36. Babenkov, Vlassov, and Poliakov: Sketch of the general plan for a new Socialist city near Novosibirsk.

181

penetrate the city from different directions. One of these will connect the old town with the new one across a newly planned bridge spanning **Fig. 36** the Ob and will touch the administrative center at the same time. The second connects the two railroad stations, while the third one leads from the main square to a so-called "food center" (see below) in the vicinity of the industrial district. Freight and truck traffic is relegated to roads outside of the city, which in turn are connected to the principal railroad lines. Traffic problems within the city are thereby considerably eased. The Center of Culture, museums, hotels, and the Central Palace of Culture are located on the fringes of the central park area, deliberately at some distance from the administrative center.

Parks are given an important place in the life of the city: they provide protection from industry and supply fresh air to the city. Apart from the sports facilities, schools and colleges will also be located in the green areas. These green belts make up 30 percent of the built-up area of the city not including the smaller tree-planted areas between the individual houses. Outside the city the plan calls for a central hospital and a number of sanatoria, one for each 110 to 125 acres.

The new plan of the city pays special attention to physical training. Sports facilities are not only attached to the communal houses, but are also placed within the park areas, which will accommodate sports centers of 4 to 4 ½ acres and include stadia of up to 10,000 capacity. The largest sports complex will be located on the shore of the Ob, easily accessible to the inhabitants of both the old and the new city. Apart from a racetrack, including racing stables, it will feature a sports palace, a stadium for 40,000 to 60,000 spectators, a swimming pool, an open-air Greek amphitheater, and many other facilities. After its completion, this boldly planned sports park will rank supreme among modern international park facilities.

The architects of this giant project have solved the question of food services by the planning of mechanized superkitchen facilities, which in general have become accepted in the USSR as an essential component of city-planning practice. These superkitchens will serve the community in the interim only, until 1944–45—this being the target date for the completion of the construction plan—at which time they will be combined into a large food commune that will eventually be located somewhere in the vicinity of the railroads, the warehouses, and the combine factory in the southeastern part of the city. The food commune should thus eventually be able to supply all inhabitants of the city with meals by the shortest possible route. It is expected that with the development of this district the center of the old city will shift and fuse with the center of the new city by means of the new bridge.

The above represents merely a rough outline of the concept of the Socialist city that is being evolved on the basis of completely new principles, unheard of so far in Western Europe and America. The old form of street blocks has been abandoned and is being replaced by linear housing interspersed with green belts—the main characteristic of the new city. It would be wrong to regard such a city as just another version of the garden city. On the contrary, the governing principle here is to include nature directly in the life of the city and to provide plenty of light and air. Still, some elements peculiar to West European architecture (Le Corbusier's *Voisin* Plan for the City of Paris has indeed exerted a wide influence on the proposals discussed above) seem to have crept in just the same. The essential difference between Socialist and Western city planning is revealed by the general uniformity of Russian city plans, based on the underlying assumption of a maximum communization of the population's mode of life. There is no passion for skyscrapers (Le Corbusier), neither are there any barrack-style residential stereotypes à la Ernst May, whose designs have been sharply criticized and rejected by the youth workers' press and the architectural societies alike. In this context, standardization is used to serve the goal of maximum comfort and expediency rather than oppressing and debasing human beings, as for instance in the case of the standardized settlements of Thomas Bata in Bohemia. The plan of Novosibirsk is a classic example of an entirely new city concept, and its realization represents one of the great events in modern architecture.

Wilm Stein: Experiment: "Socialist Cities"*

Realization of communes too expensive—therefore postponed

Moscow, April 30, 1931

In its annual budget for 1931, the Soviet Union has appropriated the huge sum of 1.1 billion rubles for residential construction, twice as much as in 1930, and it is hoped that in the year 1931 new dwelling space will be more than doubled compared to the previous year, particularly since a decree of March 1 has ordered a decrease in building costs from a prevailing average of 170 rubles per square meter (and sometimes even more) to 104 rubles per square meter.

The "third decisive year" of the Five-Year Plan—as 1931 is usually referred to in all proclamations—is among other things supposed to represent a turning point in the solution of Russia's acute housing shortage. With the exception of Leningrad, which was changed from national capital to provincial city after the Revolution, the housing shortage in the Soviet Union is very acute indeed. The influx of people into cities and workers' settlements is so great that, regardless of the yearly increase of appropriations for housing, the average living area per capita has steadily decreased during the 14 years since the Revolution. In Moscow the figure is presently approximately 4 square meters per person, while in the Don district it is 4.2 square meters per person. It should be noted that in the cities the actual average is somewhat higher for favored factory workers. In previous years, and according to plan, this segment of the population was settled by the government almost exclusively in new dwellings, while others were moved into the apartments of the former "bourgeoisie" which had been liberated by the authorities by force or otherwise. Even today some workers in Moscow occupy as little as 3 square meters per head, excluding favored groups and discounting the barracks for migrant labor.

Present conditions in the Soviet Union are so bad that even a budget of more than a billion rubles will not be enough to guarantee the solution of the housing shortage, though this will certainly ease the situation. Due to rapid industrialization, the need for housing in the industrial areas increases at a rate faster than that of even the most vigorous construction activity. For example, in the Don district the population has increased by 38 percent in the past 3 years, while living space has in-

---

* From: *Bauwelt*, XXI, Berlin 1931, pp. 703–4.

creased by only 25 percent. However, worse than the obvious lag between housing construction and population increase is the shortage of building materials, which has become increasingly acute as a consequence of expanded total building activity. In a session of the Council of the People's Commissars of April 13 it was reported that the fulfillment of the quota in the building-materials industry in the first quarter of 1931 has been "completely unsatisfactory." Figures quoted for individual plants varied from 60 to 25 percent short of the target quota. From the Don district the Moscow press reported as follows: "A threatening shortage of building materials imperils the implementation of this directive [i.e., the government's directive to build housing to the extent of 94 million rubles in this district in 1931] to its full extent and on time...." And further: "...a great number of unfinished houses often lacking roofs, floors, ceilings, doors, etc., have been carried over from the previous year into 1931 due to lumber shortages.... Some of the dwellings built remained without heating or plumbing fixtures.... These are equipped with temporary stoves only, and often lack sewage or water supply." During recent years even the best and most lavish projects in Moscow have been beset by similar obstacles. There are cases where the installation of plumbing often does not keep up with new construction, and others where the overworked railroads deliver only 1680 carloads of building materials instead of 6500 as ordered (their March quota); or where the new project cannot be delivered because no sewer, water, or heating pipes can be procured. In general it must be stated that because of shortages of material and labor, the housing program for 1930 has *not* been fulfilled. In order to carry out the much bigger program of 1931, unprecedented efforts will be required, especially since prospects for the production of some of the most important building materials (such as bricks, steel, cement, etc.) are not very favorable. During a recent session of the All-Russian Economic Council, the deputy of the Workers' Commissariat for Inspection said: "This year industry is even less prepared for the implementation of the building-materials production program than last year."

The above represents a sober assessment of the whole situation, the housing shortages, and the many other obstacles that defy solution, and also explains why, contrary to all theoretical and tactical considerations, the Communist Party and the Soviet government has had to abandon under pressure the experiment of "Socialist architecture" and "Socialist cities," at least for the foreseeable future.

The idea of "Socialist cities" has aroused interest not only in Russia and in Moscow, but all over the world. A whole new extensive literature has been devoted to this subject, and the whole concept has been explored in heated arguments, model exhibits, plans, and proposals by eminent specialists, both native and foreign. All the world was waiting for the great "new thing" that Communism would contribute to architecture. In the laboratories—meaning in the brains of artists and architects— and even in the construction offices, work goes on; but as far as practical results are concerned, we have to reconcile ourselves to the fact that the "Socialist city" is still far removed from reality and that, as far as the foreseeable future is concerned, we shall have to be satisfied with a few model projects of so-called "collective dwellings," a few functional modernistic clubs, and some communal apartment buildings that are really nothing but demeaned hotels, devoid of luxury, and modified to fit the workers' daily routine, being "Socialist collective" dwellings only in name: viz., single-bedroom apartments, common living rooms, dining halls, recreation rooms complemented by nurseries, laundries, and electric superkitchens.

Even though the idea of "Socialist cities" has not been completely renounced, any attempt to realize this concept at all in the foreseeable future has been abandoned after some long arguments among Communist thinkers, and was, in fact, formalized right in the middle of the controversy by an ukase issued on March 25 by the Central Committee of the Party. This ukase asks for "light" dwelling construction, and recommends so-called "standard construction" wherever possible for typical two- and three-family dwellings in wood, cinderblock, or other suitable material that may be available in the locality or that may be in supply at the moment. After the publication of this ukase, the Soviet press indignantly attacked all "right-wing opportunists" who for reasons of economy and expediency, and as a temporary solution, had recommended the construction of housing barracks, but castigated even more violently the "leftists" and "ultraradicals," whom they accused of espousing "gigantism" in the form of costly and enormous projects, and even though it may sound unbelievable, the party organ *Pravda* then suddenly decided to separate itself with a mighty heave from all the "wild dreamers" who dared ask for their visionary cities at once, and who advocated the "full socialization of the entire life style, the separation of children from their parents, and similar things connected with fancy project making."

All the noise is now in the direction of "standard conventional construction." The retreat from the gospel truth of "Socialist cities" to small and primitive wooden houses for which design offices supply plans and drawings in great quantities is made more palatable by daily new discoveries of the advantages of wood construction: "Standard houses do not require scarce materials such as steel and cement…. Compared to a cost of 170 rubles per square meter of masonry construction, standard house construction costs only 80 rubles per square meter." Additional advantages of traditional wood construction are quoted as follows: labor savings, savings in terms of engineers and technicians, short construction time, alleviation of railroad-transport loads, and so on. It is therefore not surprising that a resolution has already been drafted calling for a switch to wood construction in the Moscow region, in Stalingrad and, above all, in the Don district—and yes, even in the newly planned industrial city of Magnitogorsk (being planned under the supervision of the Frankfurt architect May) which had been selected from its very beginning as an example of a "Socialist model city" (in spite of the fact that even according to previous plans only 25 percent of the city was to be constructed on the basis of the so-called "collective style"). The changeover from Socialist collective cities as a symphony of steel, concrete, glass, skyscrapers, and giant clubs, to modest, small-scale residences in wood is quite a blow to Communist theory. However, it is also an indicator of a return to healthier and more sober attitudes on the part of the Soviet government, a fact which has lately been noticeable in other areas as well and which leads one to except that a way has been found out of the utopian obsession, with its wild dreams, toward more reasonable policies of economic recovery and stability. It is obvious. that the party and the government were guided in their decision to retreat from "Socialist-collective" to traditional single dwellings primarily by the idea that wood construction was much faster and considerably cheaper and that it had more chance for quick success in terms of alleviating the housing shortage. Apart from this, it should not be overlooked that the mood of the population—particularly the working population—strongly resisted collectivization; this indicates that aside from the aforementioned reasons, the retreat of the party was obviously a political device designed to reduce tensions. This was a wise move, since the failure to do so would have added another explosive item to an already explosive situation. It is no secret that the great majority of the Russian working class rejects the collective dwelling. True, the student and the young worker seem to tolerate the hotel-like regimentation, but as soon as they marry they want a "home," something "individual." Be it ever so small, it is at least their own, where they can live for themselves and their family, firmly closing the door to the outside world.

187

Ernst May, Moscow: City Building in the USSR*

City Planning in Evolution

If there is any one area of endeavor in the USSR where the Revolution is still in full motion, then city building and dwelling construction must be considered first. This is not surprising, for the replacement of a thousand-year-old social system by a new one is a process that will take more than just a dozen years to complete, or even to provide a clear and unequivocal direction. Moreover, since the thorough reorganization of the entire social life of the USSR, which covers one sixth of the land area of our globe, will vitally affect city development and housing everywhere, it follows that within the context of this general process of change it is at the present moment impossible to offer a panacea that would suddenly cure all the many ills accumulated over centuries and bring about immediate mature results.

Nevertheless, a number of theories have been advanced and are in hard competition with each other. Some of these have been published abroad, and this in turn may have led to the impression that it is only these that somehow represent the mainstream of Russian city plannig. Nothing could be more misleading!

So far there has been no firm commitment to one or the other system of city planning, and by all indications no such commitment should be forthcoming in the near future. This does not mean that the field is dominated by a lack of planning or by arbitrariness. The basic precepts of modern city planning, which in the past years have found wide acceptance in Europe, and which are now being implemented, have become the A to Z of planning in the USSR as well. Clear separation of industry and residence, rational traffic design, the systematic organization of green areas, etc., are considered as valid a basis for healthy planning there as here; similarly, open-block planning is giving way to single-row building.

The Central Problem of the Socialist City

However, even though the general principles for the planning of Socialist cities have been established, the real problem is only beginning. In other words, a city structure will have to be developed that in terms of its entire genesis as well as in terms of its internal articulation and structuring will be fundamentally different from the capitalist cities

---

* From: *Das Neue Rußland*, VIII–IX, Berlin 1931.

in the rest of the world. While our own cities in most cases owe their origin to commerce and the market place, with private ownership of land largely determining their form, the generating force behind the development of new cities in the Soviet Union is always and exclusively industrial economic production, regardless of whether in the form of industrial combines or agricultural collectives. In contrast to prevailing practice in Europe, and with particular reference to trends in the USA, building densities in Soviet cities are not influenced by artificially inflated land values, as often happens in our case, but solely by the

Fig. 37 laws of social hygiene and economy. In connection with this it should be pointed out most emphatically that the word "economy" has taken on an entirely new meaning east of the Polish border. Investments, which in the local sense may appear to be unprofitable, become con-

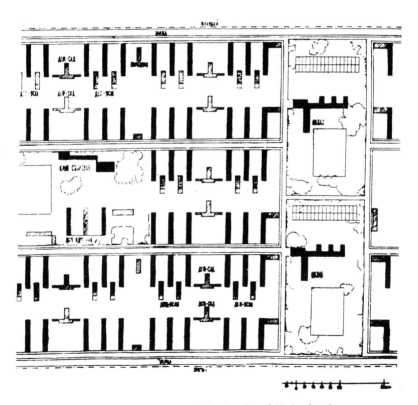

Fig. 37. Plan of a so-called "quarter" in the city of Shcheglovsk.

vincingly viable when seen from the vantage point of over all national planning by the state.

At this point I should like to point out most emphatically that among the innumerable misjudgments made abroad, none is more incorrect than that which assumes that work in the field of city planning and housing in the USSR is done without rhyme or reason, and that the ground has been cut from under their feet. The truth is that the economic and cultural reconstruction of all life in the USSR has no parallel in the history of mankind. *It is equally true that this reconstruction is being accomplished by a sober evaluation of all the realities, and it should be obvious to any observer that in each successive stage, matters recognized as desirable and ideal are being consciously subordinated to matters that are feasible and possible within the limitations of the present.* In the course of this discussion I shall return to this point on appropriate occasions.

The Over-all Form of the Socialist City

As far as the general size of the city is concerned, the decision has been made to avoid in the future urban centers with populations larger than 150,000–200,000. Reference is made to Lenin, who said: "We must aim at the fusion of industry and agriculture, based on the rigorous application of science, combined with the utilization of collective labor, and by means of a more diffused settlement pattern for the people. We must end the loneliness, demoralization, and remoteness of the village, as well as the unnatural concentration of vast masses of people in the cities."

Based on the above, the Five-Year Plan proposes decentralization of industrial production and thus automatically prevents the formation of excessive human concentrations. As mentioned earlier, opinions vary widely concerning the methods by which these new settlement policies should be implemented.

Street-Aligned Single-Story Buildings

A proposal has been advanced to construct single-story buildings on pylons à la Corbusier, placing them at certain intervals along both sides of roads leading to kolkhozes. The Soviets do not take this idea too seriously and tend to toy with it in the theoretical sense only. It has never been tried in practice, and indications are that the concept will never actually be realized; generally it must be considered exceedingly uneconomical, particularly in terms of over-all state economic planning.

190

Scattered Settlements: The Land as the Good Life

Another proposal suggests *dissolving the city* altogether. This idea is based on a proposal made by Bruno Taut some years ago, under the slogan: "The Land as the Good Life." To all intents and purposes, and as far as industrialization is concerned, this proposal will not be realized either, especially since it presupposes long traveling distances for the workers to their place of work, and also because it ignores the fact that individual agricultural land cultivation does not exist in the Soviet Union any longer, or more precisely, will no longer exist there in a few years. Another facet that is being ignored is the fact that the endeavors of the new Socialist city are inseparably bound up with the encouragement of communal life in the Socialistic sense and, furthermore, that the proposed extensive scattering of people over a large land area makes such a scheme infinitely difficult to realize.

So far only two city-planning systems incorporating general principles similar to those described above have been realized: the closed, medium-density city, and the satellite city.

The Linear City

Insofar as former is concerned—i.e., *the linear city*—and based on considerations of functionalism in planning, no other place on earth provides a better opportunity for its realization than the USSR, where industrial combines are sprouting in the desolate steppe like spring mushrooms, evolving their own particular form apparently well suited to embrace a wide range of functional requirements, such as the organization of industry according to assembly-line methods, and the settlement of large masses of people at a short distance from work.

Material concerning this and other forms of the Socialist city may be found in a book by Miliutin, entitled *The Problem of Building Socialist Cities*, to be published soon in German translation.

The linear city is structured in such a way that industry—evolving on the basis of internal organization—is arranged in a linear manner with a parallel residential development, both separated by a green belt a few hundred meters wide. The railroads are located away from the green belt on the far side of industry; this in turn compels the workers to cross the highway incorporated into the green belt while hurrying from their residences to the factories, but without having to cross the railroad tracks. As far as the question of its general form is concerned, and in cases where satellite cities (to be described later) may become impossible as a solution, the idea of linear cities is both compelling and healthy, and there is no doubt in the author's mind that it will conquer the future. Quite obviously, the linear city is to a large extent influenced by local geographical conditions. For instance, Miliutin's proposal would not work for the city of Magnitogorsk, simply because the terrain there is restricted by the 14 km-long dam on the one side and the iron-ore mountain on the other, thus precluding any kind of parallel development. Ever since autumn of last year, an intensive struggle has been going on over the issue whether the residential part of the city should be located on the other side of Ural Lake, to be connected by two bridges across the lake to the industrial development or—as my colleagues and myself have suggested—whether the city should be moved onto the high, flat plateau near the industrial sector. Two weeks ago my standpoint was definitely confirmed by a decision of the Council of People's Commissars.

Miliutin's planning proposal for the city of Stalingrad* also required considerable adjustment. Simonov's project, which is quite uneconom-ical, proposes the segmentation of the residential districts in the city into five individual communities. This would tend to move residential development too far away from industry, in turn necessitating long transportation routes through completely undeveloped territory, apart from the difficulty of having to overcome large differences in elevation between the first and the second terraces that run parallel to the Volga. Miliutin's proposal is based on a layout that separates the residential row of districts along the Volga by a park, placing industry and the railroads on the other side of the green belt. It ignores the important function of the Volga as a transportation element, for the river provides a cheap and natural means of delivery and dispatch of raw materials and finished products to and from the industrial plants that make up the 35 km-long linear city. Even before the war, a number of large industrial concerns—which in the meantime have been extensively enlarged and added to—were located along the shores of the Volga for the sole purpose of facilitating a natural turnover between the railroad lines running parallel to the river and river traffic as such.

As a result of the foregoing I based my project on the idea of the linear city, leading to the establishment of the following sequence: waterway, shore road, industry, green belt, residential belt, and the slopes of the second Volga plateau.

---

* Now Volgograd. [Tr.]

The Satellite City

As soon as the spaces separating the individual industrial sectors and their corresponding residential districts become very broad, the linear city actually changes into the last form I wish to discuss, the *satellite city*. Frequently the development of industrial groups, which have no relationship to each other and whose concentration tends to produce excessive corresponding concentrations of population, leads to satellite-like configurations around a common center serving the satisfaction of cultural and administrative needs. In a situation such as this, the individual industrial and residential groups may then be developed as relatively independent entities. I proposed such a solution for the city of Moscow, which, in spite of disastrous traffic conditions, still tends to expand in a homogeneous fashion. A similar solution has been suggested for the city of Novosibirsk on the basis of its traffic and local geographic conditions. A number of other cities have worked out similar expansion programs based on the idea of satellite cities, which have the great advantage over linear cities of allowing for possible expansion whenever there is a sudden need for unexpected growth. The linear city as such represents a closed system, in most cases quite incapable of incorporating any kind of expansion element into its structure organically or, at best, rendering such an expansion extremely difficult.

Fig. 38. General plan of the city of Magnitogorsk.

The Structure of the Socialist City

I shall now attempt to articulate the inner structure of the Socialist city. It is a declared aim of the Soviet political system to put the energies of all citizens capable of work in the service of the state—men and women alike. Communism considers it a waste of valuable time and out of tune with modern life to see the function of woman in terms of lifelong cooking and dusting, when she should be contributing both physically and intellectually to the common good, using her free time to cultivate both body and mind. Actually, such a view merely expresses the thoughts of hundreds of thousands, nay millions, of progressive individuals in all parts of the world. As far as the full mobilization of all the total working force is concerned, this is not really a pressing problem in capitalist countries, particularly in the face of their present catastrophic unemployment, which has forced this issue very much into the background. Conditions in the USSR are quite different. When the Russian delegate in Geneva was recently offered a post on a commission that was to concern itself with the problem of unemployment, he coupled his acceptance with the remark that the Union which he represented was not faced with this problem.

Among the many measures designed to alleviate the problem of labor shortage, the most important is the *utilization of the woman labor force*. Specifically, what does this mean? It means that all those functions that until now have been carried out by women in the household—or at least the largest part of these functions—will have to be taken over by public agencies: among these are first and foremost the functions of *food supply* and *child rearing*. As far as the problem of *public food preparation* is concerned, no major difficulties seem to block the way. The large public kitchens in Moscow, Leningrad, and numerous other centers of industrial and agricultural developments have proven quite successful, even though there are definite tendencies toward overcrowding in some of these establishments. Smaller dining facilities, which tend to facilitate a certain amount of personal contact between consumer and producer, are preferred. The planning of new cities in the USSR calls for the construction of so-called food combines, which, when fully equipped, will contain slaughterhouses, bread factories, storehouses, and superkitchens for the production of semi-finished food products. In turn these will be delivered to the various consumer outlets in the residential districts.

Much more difficult than the problem of food distribution is that of *child rearing*. The question is being dealt with in a systematic way.

People brought up in the capitalistic part of the world usually have the following question on the tip of their tongue: "What happens to *their* family life?" I answer this question by asking: "What has happened to *our* family life?"

Regrets or no regrets, the fact remains that the traditional image of the family is in the process of extinction. Our youth find no pleasure in wasting their time in instructive conversations with aunties and uncles, particularly when their time can be much better spent in the systematic cultivation of their minds and bodies or in the company of members of their own age group. Many people will admit that much, but they will hesitate to admit that their wives are in fact being communized, even in cases where this has become an actual fact without their recognizing it as such.

Fig. 39. General plan of the city of Tirgan.

I do not wish to dwell on this subject any longer, but just the same **Fig. 39**
I would like to point out that my personal impression is that hypocrisy
in the USSR in all matters of sex is being condemned, and that
in terms of purity and natural morality its standards are on an
exceptionally high level, unknown to us. The relationship between
man and woman in the context of collective life has been left
untouched and is being regarded as a strictly private affair between
individuals. This leaves us to investigate the relationship between
parents and children. In this area the last word has not yet been spoken.
The extreme radicals demand a complete separation of children from
their parents at the earliest age. Fed in child-care centers, instructed
in play in kindergartens, and brought up in boarding schools and
dormitories, they are to develop separate from adults. In reality there
is indeed a compelling need to relieve the working mother from the
worries of child rearing. However, attempts are being made to achieve
this in a different manner, whereby children are put into nurseries
during the work day and are brought up normally by their parents
during the rest of the time; this is indeed very similar to our system.
For working mothers with babies requiring nursing, crèches and
nurseries fulfill the same function. These will have to be established in
the large factories as well, so as to allow their mothers to participate
fully in the activities of the Komsomol.

Three Housing Categories

Presently three housing types are being developed along parallel lines,
depending on whether one takes a radical or moderate view of the
problem. It is as yet impossible to say that a clear decision has been
made for any of the three types, even though it is becoming increasingly
evident that the general thrust will be in the direction of an intensive
promotion of a collective style of life, especially for the coming
generation, which finds the purest embodiment of this aspiration in
the institution of the Komsomol.

The 100-percent Private Dwelling

The term "moderates" includes those people who even now still "own"
their *individual homes* in the truest sense of the word. Their right to
private ownership is based on a law of 1918, which made an exception
to the wholesale land expropriation by the state for small one-family
houses with a value of less than 10,000 rubles; these were allowed to
remain the private property of their owners. Such families live as we

196

do, with one possible difference that is not unimportant, namely, the combination of these housing districts with "people's houses", or clubs as they are called in the USSR, which provide the focal point for all community life in these settlement groups. The children are brought up at home as before, except in cases where there are kindergartens close by to accommodate them.

The Collective House
The next group is the class of so-called *collective houses*, or *obieshidie*. These are used by people who have given up the use of private kitchens, and who now take their meals in group kitchens on the individual floors of the building or in public dining facilities serving the whole district. Babies up to three years of age are taken care of in district nurseries, and 3- to 7-year-olds are accommodated by district kindergartens, usually during the parents work hours. School education for the children is similar to our mode of public education.

The Communal House
The most radical form of dwelling is the *communal house*, i.e., a structure accommodating an optimum of approximately 400 people or, if two elements are combined, 800 people, and forming a complete dwelling community. Each individual has a living area of 6 to 9 square meters for his own personal use. In other words, a childless married couple would occupy a space of 12 square meters. This space is used for sleeping, reading, writing, and other strictly private functions. In some of the more ideal projects one shower per two rooms will be provided as an added feature. All other aspects of life are collective, and all meals are taken in common dining halls. At most, a small heating unit is provided on each floor for the preparation or warming up of snacks, etc. Work and play take place in common club rooms. Babies are nursed in a separate nursery, connected to the main building by a closed corridor, and older children are accommodated day and night in kindergartens built for this purpose. Children of school age sleep in school dormitories.

The Financing of Public Education
The foregoing brings up the extremely complicated *problem of financing* and leads to the question of whether such a system of housing and education will not eventually turn out to be more expensive than private education. In reply it must be noted that final figures have not

been made available to date and probably will not be available for some time to come. However, some of the available cost estimates permit us to say that expenditures for these service structures described do not result in an over-all increase in cost, provided they represent an equivalent quantity withdrawn from the individual apartment areas. This leaves the question of maintenance and operating costs. This can only be resolved in estimating the useful labor being gained by freeing women from household work, since only approximately one half of the women released from household chores will be required to serve in the communal facilities.

Real Housing Policies

When I mentioned earlier that the policies of responsible agencies in the USSR remain firmly anchored in reality and are far removed from any indulgence in politics of illusion, then this applies above all to the problem of housing. In centers of industrial reconstruction, such as Magnitogorsk and Kuznetsk, and in the mighty push to accommodate 700,000 miners with their families by December 31 of the current year, 75 percent of the housing will consist of individual dwellings, and only 25 percent will be collective and/or communal housing.

The Structure of the Socialist City

On the basis of the foregoing evidence you may be able to gain a broad overview of the organic development of the city, which I will now briefly retrace. While the capitalist city has developed concentrically around the market place, and while the rich, the middle classes, and the proletarians live in clearly separated districts of their own—this differentiation of class structure being recognizable from afar and defining the capitalist city's peculiar character and form—the city in the USSR knows only one class, the class of the working people. Therefore, apart from the aforementioned requirement of locating people as close as possible to their respective places of work, the task consists in the equitable distribution of all communal functions, for everybody's equal enjoyment. In other words, nurseries, kindergartens, schools, stores, laundries, ambulances, hospitals, clubs, cinemas, and other facilities should be apportioned in such a manner as to be within a comfortable and functionally optimum distance from the dwellings.

Naturally there may be a number of different solutions to satisfy these conditions. During the planning of the city of Magnitogorsk two schemes finally emerged from among the others for comparison and evaluation. The proposal by Chernichev suggested a tripartite division of the city and provided each separate part with its own center; the proposal advanced by myself in collaboration with my closest associates was based on the principle that the Socialist city must be conceived in terms of conceptual unity, and we rejected the three-part segmentation of the other scheme as being arbitrary, demanding instead the creation of organizational elements that would be made operative by the propitious use of communal service facilities.

My proposal calls for units of 8000–10,000 population, the so-called "quarters." The Commission of the Sovnarkom, which was asked to make the final decision, decided to select my proposal. It has become the basis of all other projects undertaken with my assistance.

City Building and Cost

Considering the billions that the USSR is investing not only in building up its industry but also in the cities attached to that industry, and further considering that these sums do not come from loans but out of current income, it may be interesting to find out to what degree the problem of city-development costs has been solved there, keeping in mind that in the old world this problem has so far remained almost completely unsolved. In the previously mentioned book by Miliutin, a short chapter entitled "Approximate Development Costs" deals with the essentials of new city financing, based on a program prepared by the State Economic Planning Agency "GOSPLAN." In order to arrive at a broader picture, these estimates should also include the cost of all public buildings, food combines, transportation facilities, etc., so as to provide the reader with a more complete summary of the total cost of the Socialist city. Furthermore, this figure should be complemented by a comparable parallel cost estimate for the industrial base, while a deduction of operating costs and interest on capital for city development from their proceeds may give us something resembling a first rough estimate of the cost of the Socialist city.

Before going on, it should be pointed out that the emphasis is on "something resembling"; for at the present no precise figures are available and probably will not be available in the near future. However, we do know that in the USSR expenditures for development of the Socialist city run somewhere between $250 and $350 per capita, assuming parity between the ruble and the dollar. As long as the tempo of work maintains its frantic pace, and as long as some of the obstacles—to be described below in detail—are not removed, cost accounting will have to continue on the basis of rough estimates rather than on the basis of mathematical and scientific accuracy, with the concomitant danger of both major and minor departures from reality.

Development Obstacles

The Five-Year Plan of the USSR is indeed a grandiose venture, and one cannot but admire its clear objectives and the forthright way chosen to achieve its goals. However, any account would remain one-sided if the enormous difficulties that must be overcome to fulfill the plan were left unmentioned, particularly those in the area of building construction. Earlier I mentioned the acute shortage of manpower, above all skilled labor, capable of carrying out the necessary intensive work. I am not even thinking of technical personnel, which could possibly be upgraded by the rational enlistment of the talent now concentrated in the big cities—this no doubt will be done eventually—but I am speaking of the most primitive class of labor, meaning workers doing the digging, bricklaying, carpentry, etc. The new labor force now migrating into the industrial centers is drawn primarily from the rural population. These people, as is well known, still live on a very low level of cultural development, especially those coming from some of the more remote provinces. If one wishes to judge conditions in the USSR fairly, one must keep in mind that it may be quite easy to civilize countries of the size of Germany, Austria, or Italy, but it will require a generation of virtually superhuman effort to push even the most elementary principles of human civilization to the shores of the Arctic Ocean and the Mongolian border.

The human problem is matched in magnitude and importance only by the transportation problem. In many respects the Soviet Union of today may be compared to a capitalist real-estate holder who has many valuable assets in his possession but is unable to put them into use and is thus subject to a feeling of abject poverty.

Vast resources are hidden throughout the land, beginning with platinum and gold, and ending with wood and coal; their presence has been explored and is a matter of record. However, a look at a map will reveal that hardly any transportation lines exist in the Asiatic part of the USSR. The only exceptions are the Great Siberian Main Line, a few smaller branch lines, and the new Turksib Line. All other transport moves laboriously by river, small carts, or sledges. The hectic work pace after the war hardly allowed time for the maintenance and replacement of existing railroad facilities; few them were in first-class condition to begin with. As a result of all this, the transportation and handling of the enormous quantities of goods to be shipped has become a serious problem.

Hardly less of a problem is the *shortage of important building materials* resulting from the general neglect of industrial development in prewar Russia, which failed to establish a building-materials industry of sufficient capacity. As a consequence of all this, the USSR is presently faced by the enormously difficult task of having to develop programs for both industry and agriculture on an unprecedented scale, while at the same time having to produce out of thin air factories that will provide the basic production facilities for construction and building materials. Steel, glass, roof-covering materials, cement, and many other items have been placed on so-called lists of deficit materials and may be used in domestic construction only in very special cases.

For this reason a number of directives and regulations have recently been published, containing the most stringent measures concerning the economic use of materials, and prescribing the most intensive utilization of available local materials. A clear recognition of essentials gives first priority to industrial construction in both city and country, while housing is relegated to second place.

The Big Push: 700,000 Dwelling Units Before December 31

Given all of this, the reader should be able to appreciate what it means to organize the undertaking presently being carried out under my supervision in response to a resolution of the Council of People's Commissars, as well as in response to the personal initiative of Stalin. *It calls for the housing of 700,000 workers and their families by December 31 of the current year.*

Special consideration is to be given to the Don Basin, the Kuznetsk Basin, the Urals, and Karaganda.

To conclude my remarks, I should like to give you a small overview of one sector of this crash program, namely the organization of a group of 250,000 dwelling units in the Donets District:

All the work is carried out on the basis of the *most radical standardization and modular coordination* of the whole building process. While a group of twenty architects visited the 150 buildings sites in the Donets District, choosing and surveying sites according to previously prepared directives, the central agency drew up plans and designs for typical housing units, to be assembled later on the sites selected. Fifteen different dwelling types have been developed, most of them consisting of large, standardized units produced by the big Russian lumber works, and ready for final assembly on the site. In the factory each piece is stamped with a number and the designation of its location. This prevents confusion during transport and assembly. A special Building Materials Department organizes the delivery of materials, and local supervision is carried out by a *special building trust* (*Donshilstroi*), created for this very purpose. The headquarters of this whole trust is in the Ukrainian city of Kharkov, with branches in the six main regions of the territory. These branches in turn maintain a number of District Construction Offices, each charged with the supervision of five or six settlement sites.

I mentioned earlier that there is a shortage of certain building materials, as for example roofing. Using a well-equipped laboratory in Moscow, we are trying to find substitutes for these shortages. A number of highly qualified scientists are contributing to this effort. In order to control speed and quality of construction, the following three procedures have been initiated. A schedule of target dates has been prepared for each construction site. Progress is checked in the office of the Ukrainian headquarters by a scanning of telegraphic reports submitted each 3–5 day period. These reports are in turn checked against a copy of the construction schedule. Three so-called *control brigades*, using automobiles, speed from site to site, checking compliance with technical directives as well as the rational organization of construction. Finally, the production manager and his staff make surprise control visits. Action in the Urals, the Moskva Basin, and the Kuznetsk Basin is organized along similar lines. It goes without saying that extreme flexibility of organization must be tolerated to offset the existence of the many difficulties mentioned above. *We strive for the impossible while achieving the possible.*

Conclusion

In Moscow, only the day before yesterday I boarded the international train that had just arrived from Harbin and made my way to the dining car. There I noticed a very un-English Englishman, who was busying himself by going from table to table, pointing at small blemishes on the table cloths and repeating in a nasal voice: "Oh, how dirty!" He is going to say nasty things about Russia. I too saw these blemishes; in fact I saw much bigger ones and others that were far more serious. I saw the difficulties in the area of nutrition that exist in certain localities; I saw the poorly maintained buildings in the large cities; and I also noticed the ugly impulse toward bureaucratization in the USSR, which—by the way—may eventually become one of the best arguments for opening up the official pipelines of international understanding. *In spite of all this, it is impossible to deny that what is being accomplished there at this moment in time cannot be called anything but a historic act.*

I am pleased that the Congress for New Construction has decided to hold its next year's meeting in the USSR. Its participants will have an opportunity to form their own judgments about the achievements and the work accomplished there, and may be able to report to all countries what they have seen. This may also help remove many of the prejudices that obstruct international understanding and peaceful cooperation among nations.

Martin Wagner, Berlin: Russia Builds Cities*

Irony of fate! On the very day on which more than 1000 city planners published an obituary over the corpse of the European city after five days of post mortem examinations, and after concluding the session with a powerless "We can't do it!," City Engineer Ernst May (retired) delivered his grand report on Russian city building to a group of enthusiastic young architects and curious builders. The plans shown by May, his verbal commentary, the form of his lecture, and his undaunted and fresh intellect cannot in themselves account for the excitement and inner tension that gripped the whole audience. The young architects must have felt instinctively that a new life was being created in Russia, that opportunities were developing and accomplishments were maturing there, and that the creativity of the urbanist, freed from the shackles of private land ownership, was being given full reign in that country. Anticipation of the future, the feeling of liberation after long, frustrating stagnation, the letting in of sun and fresh air into a dark musty workroom—these explain why May's lecture became such an extraordinary event for the people of Berlin.

Within the framework of these presentations I cannot make it my task to offer a simple appreciation of the liberating influence of Russian urbanism as such. On the basis of my personal convictions, and also from the viewpoint of the reader, it would be more important to obtain an understanding of the *constructive ideas* of Russian planning.

National Planning

In the lexicon of German planners, "national planning" is a very pretentious word. It is much bandied about, even though everybody knows full well that true national planning is impossible without the hotly disputed econo-political *"planned economy,"* i.e., an economy serving all and satisfying the needs of all. The Russian Five-Year Plan has created, for the first time in the history of city development, the conditions for rational economic planning on a national scale. I admit that I do not really know whether all the conditions for national economic planning are being fully exploited in that country. But I do know that these conditions do not exist in any other European country, and that preparations for national planning have been advanced there

---

* From: *Tagebuch*, XXX, Berlin, July 25, 1931.

beyond the most daring dreams of our own German planners. During my short study visit to Moscow, the director of the Public Bank (which is responsible for the financing of all the newly planned Russian cities) showed me thick portfolios of planning documents for each new city to be built, complete with economic surveys, tables, soil tests, climatic charts, raw-material inventories, traffic studies, and so on. Even though I was in no position to check the content and the specific accuracy of these documents, I should like to stress the fact of the existence of such studies, and ask the German city planner when and where has he ever been supplied by a central Council of Economic Policies with action directives as part and parcel of a meaningful national plan for his city-expansion programs, together with an approved budget and, in addition, a timetable for the execution of the building schedule? We look at planning as the theory of one generation to be passed on to the next generation. In Russia, planning has become a task for the present.

Similarly, it is fully within the spirit of broadly based Russian state planning to create only functional cities of limited size (100,000 to a maximum of 200,000 population), designed to support the extraction and treatment of raw materials, or for the production of consumer goods for a region. How grateful we would be if we too had the opportunity to convert the existing system of mutually competing cities, with their near-insane propensities to run idle and to squander wealth, into well-planned components of a major central and a minor regional consumer economy. The Ruhr valley is bleeding to death due to the competition from the Upper Silesian and Central German soft-coal districts. These in turn are so inefficient that even coal imported from England is cheaper, putting the German miner out of work and adding to our problem of unemployment. Our *Reichswirtschaftsrat* (State Economic Council) knows all these problems but is unable to solve them, simply because its competence stops short of the provincial boundaries, and because it has absolutely no power to extend its planning to county territory or beyond the various other local boundaries of jurisdiction. National planning in this country will remain an illusion as long as there is no State Economic Council with full jurisdiction over the territory of the whole nation and all its natural resources.

State planning is the fountainhead of the science of Russian Urban Economic Planning and all economic practice. The knowledge of these matters is still too limited in Western Europe to form any kind of definite value judgment, except in a vague, general way.

Obviously rational, centrally directed state planning has not only positive aspects, but negative ones as well, particularly if it fails to avoid the danger of bureaucratic bungling and ill-considered, hasty investments. Considering the unilateral single-use character of their cities, a miscalculation could very easily lead to investment errors and possibly to a loss of the entire capital input, which for a city of 100,000 population represents a national loss of the sizeable sum of half a billion marks. Even though—in contrast to all other cities in the world—the Russian cities base their cost figures on the complete balance of expenditures over cost, and even though they are being financed out of current income, the national economy has to be charged forthwith with an amount of equal value, for the simple reason that the state—in contrast to private-enterprise capitalism—has the obligation to provide an alternative settlement for 100,000 people in another location. *Careful budgetary planning of all these functional cities is therefore the first condition of rational national planning.*

The second great advantage of Russian national planning is the fact that the Soviets have the opportunity to develop their relatively new and undeveloped transportation network on the basis of purely economic considerations. Unlike ourselves, they do not have to connect old historic localities, that have lost their economic reason for existence and that only dream about the glories of the past, to the existing railroad network, and thereby unnecessarily overload the-over all system. Russia has the opportunity to develop its transportation system on the basis of schedules of departure, arrival, transfer, and intersection of transport, all related to city function and in accordance with the principles of maximum efficiency and economy of plant and equipment, and avoid the wasted trips so dreaded by transportation experts. For example, some of the iron ore from the new mining and smelting center in Magnitogorsk is sent to the coal and refining city of Kuznetsk 2000 kilometers away. There, the same wagons are loaded with coal and returned to Magnitogorsk to smelt part of the iron ore on the spot. Thus, the national transportation system is clearly being treated as part of a single, over-all national industrial complex, which in turn is being treated as a large-scale service city, and both transportation and industry are made to fit organically within the general context of the economy. When industry prospers, so do the railroads, and vice versa. This represents the most important advantage of such a system but could also turn into one of the most evident disadvantages of such specialized plant development and of the service cities connected to it.

In the light of the foregoing, one may well ask whether it would not be more advantageous to consider industrially diversified cities instead. Definitely not. The loss of markets for raw materials, semi-finished, and finished goods in our own diversified cities has been matched by a corresponding reduction of rolling stock on the part of the Reichsbahn. Besides, the Russian consumption economy has the means of preventing excessive fluctuations in the economy or at least of achieving speedy adjustment. Should such an adjustment prove impossible, the new Russian system will have to accommodate itself to an occasional, shall we say, "locking up of a city" along with its idle industrial plant. To me the abandonment of one segment of the vast Russian economy still seems more economical than our own compulsion to put whole villages and cities on relief, rendering unemployed all those whose main source of economic life has happened to dry up at the present. Our glass industry is a good example of this.

Regional Planning
In Germany, and in other countries as well, a certain hostility persists between the country and the cities which historically developed as fortified market centers during the Middle Ages. This split is evident even in our day and age and has had many political and economic consequences, which in turn prevent the emergence of rational regional planning. New Russian planning should take note and remember that it will be dealing with the creation of cities for a rural rather than urban people.

Within the perimeters of a large-scale consumption economy geared to the supply of all basic needs to the people, it is impossible to imagine that these cities could be planned and built without providing each with its own appropriate agricultural territory for food supply. Even today there are in Germany some planners and professors of city planning who ignore the fact that the suburban fringes that surround our cities in ever widening circles—particularly the larger cities—change the character of the agricultural areas nearby. These become more and more dependent on the cities for their consumer needs and, as a corollary of this, increasingly accept urban values. Those who take the trouble to investigate agricultural operations around the cities in terms of size, production, and prices over a long period of time, ought not to be very surprised to find that the influence of the cities on the agricultural sector is much stronger than is usually assumed.

207

It took centuries of urban development to overcome the obstacles of tradition, hereditary succession, and special economic interests and to arrive at the organic interplay of exchange of goods between city and country. In contrast to this, Russia has had only a few years to create such a relationship for its service cities. Here, city planning becomes synonymous with regional planning and has a direct influence on the agricultural hinterland—something hardly imaginable in German circumstances. The Russian city has fused agriculture and urbanization into an organic whole.

The question is how to deal with this whole in a planned manner? How much does the city planner know about agriculture and the soil? Who tells him that the daily deliveries of milk, vegetables, and so forth, must be incorporated into the urban transportation system, and that he must furthermore take care of agricultural staples coming from distant production areas to a different *locus* in the transportation network? How will he know what quantities of foodstuffs will be consumed fresh or from the warehouses? All these questions direct our attention to a field of endeavor that up to now has never been elaborated by German planners on a responsible and rational economic basis, and it also shows us to what degree planners will have to adapt themselves to their new role as managers, since the Russian city planner, compared with his German counterpart, is even less in a position to combine in one person all the special knowledge required for all the various branches of regional planning.

Russian regional planning offices have nothing whatever in common with comparable German agencies—if for no other reason than that they produce practical realizations rather than paper solutions. Each Russian planning office is part of the National Economic Council, which has three subdivisions. The first is responsible for working out the economic production program for the new cities, together with a detailed budget prepared in advance. This program is transferred to the second branch, the Planning Division, which deals with the technical design and details of the city plan. The third, the Executive Division, is responsible for actual *construction*. Thus, the Russian planner cannot avoid being a manager presiding over various specialists and being responsible for a consistent policy in terms of economic performance as well as design quality. What German city builder—or rather city planner, since we have never had any real city builders in Germany—would not be enthusiastic at the chance to be the manager under circumstances that would allow him to work out a performance program for a new city already in the economic planning stage? In Russia an urban community is designed and evaluated on the basis of give and take, debit and credit—something regarded as virtually impossible in our country. Bold visions of new goals and new standards arouse our imagination.

We have become accustomed to the notion that the so-called "organic" growth of our cities, fed by an inorganic and chaotic economic system, represents a God-given untouchable "expediency." In this respect, and among other things, city caricatures such as New York convince us that such developments are anything but economical. Planners must begin to think about the economic budgeting of cities and must demand that just as in the case of any individual or any other economic enterprise, cities should not drain off our national wealth, but should on the contrary increase it. But how much do we really know about national economic budgeting for our cities even today? Officially only those statistics that do not probe too deeply into the secrets of private companies are applied to production, commerce, and consumption. This makes it impossible to set up any kind of realistic economic budget for the cities.

City Planning

The German city planner would be surprised no end if he could watch his Russian colleague at work. What! No twenty regulations, laws, and restrictions obstructing rational planning in a spiderweb of private property lines? Really free land? And no twenty-four municipal authorities who must be consulted each time the planner wishes to establish a building line? No jurisdictions, and no hangovers, and what has been planned can really be built? And the results to be really seen and experienced? No building inspectors and by-laws to obstruct free design? Indeed, under such conditions, city planning becomes a joy. And one may ask what happens to all the physical and mental exertions that are usually spent in fighting the hydra of bureaucracy, officialdom, and the law.

This comparison is not a dream, but has become reality and leads us to the conviction that the work of our German city planners is 90 percent nonproductive and useless. But it would be wrong to regard the work of the Russian city planner, free from all nonessential, formalities and the concern for private property, as child's play. Only by freeing the best creative energies of the city planner from the shackles of private property restrictions can their full flowering in their entire social, technical, and artistic dimension be assured. In our country, city planning is what the word says: mere city *planning*. In Russia city planning is in fact city *building*.

The Russian city builder is faced by a task that has not been faced by humanity during the past one thousand years: the creation of entirely new Socialist cities! It is therefore not surprising that in striving to reach such a remote goal opinions will differ and often tend to degenerate into fathomless theories. Yet realistic plans that are both pragmatic and feasible, such as those of my colleague Ernst May, are suddenly criticized by the usually objective editor, Paul F. Schmidt (in *Der Abend* of June 9, 1931), as follows: "Like a steel straightjacket, the plans of these cities and dwellings force all their inhabitants into a soul-less sameness. These are cities for slaves of the state, forbidden to lead their own lives, and their existence has only one purpose: to work like coolies for the state and to bear children." When I read these lines, I could not help but think of how very comfortable our own Socialists must feel in the "steel straightjacket" of the Wilhelmian city with its slum apartments and rear-alley catacombs, if they dare to reject the liberating influence of the urban plans and housing concepts of May, an influence that must be clearly evident to anyone who dares remain objective.

Let me concede one thing to Paul Schmidt, albeit on a different level of criticism and unencumbered by partisan and political considerations. I do admit (and so does May) that the formal layout of his new cities has not yet been "solved," in the sense that they cannot yet be considered free from ingrained design habits and traditional preconceptions. I do not wish to imply by this remark that I subscribe to the view that Socialism must inevitably produce a special art form of its own, i.e., some kind of pure "Socialist art." Anyone believing such a thing has no real conception either of art or Socialism. Still, the Russian cities will eventually evolve their own form, fit to contain life and at the same time have spiritual significance. The deepest and loftiest aspirations of the Socialist spirit must find their expression here. There is no more powerful message to the people than stone transformed into plastic form. No loudspeaker, and not even the most forceful orator can speak to the nation more consistently and convincingly, crossing generations, educating them and winning their allegiance, than a building or a city. The power of artistic accomplishment was, is, and will forever remain the work of talented great artists, of whom the world has really never produced more than a dozen in a thousand years. The creation of the Socialist city as an art form, a kind of "cathedral" of the people and Socialism is a task still to be accomplished by the Russians of the future.

Housing

The Socialist mode of dwelling is a particularly controversial subject in present-day Russia. I shall refrain from making any kind of judgment as to how many square meters of living space a citizen should be entitled to. This question is the exclusive competence of each nation's gross national product and not a matter of good or bad intentions on the part of economic planners or budget secretaries. Considering the fact that Russia made the audacious leap from a rural mode of existence to an urban one, any objective evaluation of Russian housing conditions must take into account the fact that it is impossible to increase the per capita living area from 3 square meters to 12 and 24 square meters in a couple of years, while creating a rich industrial base at the same time. What form Russian housing will take, however, is a different question. At this point I should like to state most emphatically that neither the city planner nor a political program can invent *the* Socialist form of dwelling. On the contrary, I believe that the new form of dwelling can develop only out of a variety of forms. If that is correct, then Russia seems to be on the right path, having allowed the development of the individual single-family dwelling alongside the hotel type of dwelling and the rental apartment, including a rich combination of all, and having left it to the future—say one generation—to write off some of these types and replace them with improved versions. However, it seems to me that one particular dwelling type has been largely neglected in the new plans. I refer to the traditional native Russian standard wooden house in the form of the single family type of dwelling. A nation that is as close to the soil and the open country as the Russians will always want to return, in one way or the other, to the soil, the garden, and the natural life. Because of the above, I am inclined to believe that the development of this particular Russian housing type will succeed, insofar as material improvements will tend to push expansion in the direction of a natural horizontal building development (gardens, automobiles, etc.), rather than in the direction of vertical building forms, which are the result of high land prices invented by the "landlords," and which are based on methods of stacking, attaching, and combining units above, below, and along the terrain.

211

The basic life cell of the Socialist city is the individual dwelling unit. The more the city planner gets involved with the communal functions of the city and the institutions serving mental and physical culture and away from concerns of the individual dwelling, the more insecure will be the spiritual foundations of his efforts. On the other hand it is precisely these communal areas that in essence represent a new contribution to Socialist city planning. As a Socialist I should like to go even further: it is precisely here that we find all that has yet to be expressed and translated into form, for here the relationship between one individual and the next will find its great counterform to all matters material, physical, and unconscious, creating a spirit of the larger community and a higher consciousness that in the past had found its artistic outlet in large religious communities, temple cities, monasteries, and the cathedrals.

Indeed, one may ask, what edifices of specific spiritual and cultural content have been created by capitalist Europe to date? And where can we find an expression or a forum of the community capable of transforming beautiful sights and sounds into deeper inner experience? They simply don't exist. There are some fragments, such as a kindergarten, a school of gymnastics, a theater, a meeting place, the rhythm of work, a little bit here, and a little bit there, but nowhere in its mature form. What a task for the city builder! For the sake of such a monumental task he should be given time; time to send out his emissaries to collect all the material needed for the construction of this great spiritual edifice. For the sake of this task he should be given the means to plan, to experiment, and to design. For the sake of this task he should be released from the petty annoyances of the work day, to be able to devote all his time and his best talents to accomplishing this great mission.

These communal centers will prove the physical and spiritual superiority of the Socialist cities of Russia over the capitalist cities of Europe.

Hannes Meyer, Moscow: Construction, Construction Workers, and Technicians in the Soviet Union*

Based on a lecture by Hannes Meyer, former Bauhaus director, now architect in Moscow, and was presented on October 13, 1931, in Berlin.

Hearing an architect speak conjures up the image of someone belonging to the intellectual and financial milieu of the middle classes, whose role in Western culture has been to act as an acrobat swinging between the banks and the land speculators, between bureaucrat and builder, and between the future tenant and the owner of the building to be constructed. This juggling act consumes 90 percent of his work activity, and only during the remaining 10 percent is he allowed to deal with architecture as an art. Compared to this, the position of the architect in the Soviet Union is quite different. In the Soviet Union architects are worker-builders in the front ranks of the Five-Year Plan—the *Piatiletka*. We have joined this work-battle in the ranks of the worker-builders, as officers of the technical cadres. In the sense that we are worker-builders, we see ourselves as architectural trade unionists. My union card has the number 629-828. We belong to the working classes as scientists and practical builders, and all of us together contribute to the building of the new Socialist economy. We have many jobs. For instance, I am being used by the "Institute for the Construction of Technical Colleges in the Soviet Union," (Giprovtus), for city planning (Giprogor), and in the Institute for Housing. Apart from these, I teach at the School of Architecture (Wasi) in Moscow, while at the same time I am involved in the construction of the House of Soviet, the Theater for the Masses, the House of Books, the National Publishing House (which has an annual publishing output of 12 million volumes), the Lenin School, the Communist Academy, etc. We work in teams, doing all work collectively; "personality" is not important; each of us is only one atom among a thousand others. We are attempting to significantly increase the number of students. To become a student is a distinction and not, as in Western Europe, a privilege. Whoever distinguishes himself in his work in the factories is sent to college. Students do not lead the kind of life current in the West but contribute in a productive way to the building of

* From: *Das Neue Rußland*, VIII–IX, Berlin 1931.

213

Socialism. The type of student known in the West does not exist here. We consider the student a worker. A student receives the same wage that a worker does. Studying is considered productive labor, just as productive as work done in the factory.

Education in the Soviet Union is a matter of national planning. We are being urged to let the students continue with their work in the factories. Students form groups of 4 or 5 comrades. Their slogan is "Away with individualism in education, forward with collective training!" During the first semester the student joins an existing group whose older students act as senior members. Our goal is not only to improve education in general, but to mobilize all teaching efforts. The number of teachers needed for this task is extremely high. So far, great shortages still exist in this field. Our students receive thorough instruction in the ideas of Marxism, Leninism, and Stalinism. In this way the thesis of Socialism receives its theoretical foundation. The knowledge of the average student in this area is enormous. Another important point in our system of education is strong specialization within the various professions. We are training four categories of architects: the fields of agriculture, industry, housing, and civic building. During his four years of study, each student spends 90 days in military service. In the normal course of their studies all students take military science. There is a basic identity between the state and the student. The Red Army soldier not only protects his homeland in the event of danger, but represents a great cultural force as well. All students serve in the capacity of technical cadre personnel. Our schools are not just places of education, but workshops; in fact, factories. The school as such is only an appendage; lately we have stopped the building of schools and have transferred instruction into the factories: no more workshops without a technical cadre, and no more factories without a school.

There are four different types of schools in the Soviet Union: the Workers' Faculties, the Factory Schools, the Technical Schools, and the Technical Colleges. Take the case of a former monastery located 30 kilometers outside of Moscow. The complex now accommodates 1200 students (age 10 to 27). They were picked off the streets from all over the Soviet Union (and speak many different languages). These students have formed a community of their own. In fact, the school does everything on its own. Both a public school and a technical school have been started there. Even at nine in the evening, 60 percent of the students still labor in work brigades. The students are completely free to decide all matters on their own. The founder of the school is the GPU.

The GPU has accomplished remarkable feats in the areas of education and the development of Socialism.

In the Soviet Union the factory replaces the family in almost all respects. The factory takes care of everything; it is the center of our collective existence. The office worker is in no way different from his comrade on the construction site. The chasm between worker and scientist has ceased to exist.

Still, money is important. Any banker will tell you that the ruble is worth 2.15 German marks at the border. But things are really somewhat different: the more proletarian one lives over there, the more valuable the ruble becomes. Example: in a factory a rich, full meal (soup, main course, dessert, bread, and tea) costs 38 kopecks. The same meal in a club (except for some differences in service) costs 1.5 rubles, and in a hotel such a dinner may cost as much as 6, 8, or even 10 rubles. The same goes for apartments. In this connection I would like to caution all those who apply for positions as specialists in the Soviet Union not to exert themselves for high wages. My colleagues and I went simply as comrades. We receive the same pay as our Russian comrades (300 rubles for beginners, 400 rubles for experienced workers). For foreign architects it is at first quite difficult to make ends meet on such a wage. The Russians were aware of this and in the beginning paid us 50 rubles more "for mistakes," as they put it, for it seems that these cannot be avoided in the early stages of the game.

The *building* of cities is accomplished in the Soviet Union within the over-all framework of the Five-Year Plan. Education, work, housing, and even recreation (the Park of Culture in Moscow is four kilometers long!): in short, everything is done according to plan and collectively. The construction of whole new cities, as described by May, represents the "cake," so to speak. Our "daily bread," however, consists in rebuilding existing cities. The most difficult problems have to be solved in this context. For instance, there is a city near Samarkand, a cotton center. The city has to be transformed into an industrial center. It represents a city type that over the centuries has evolved along the lines of hereditary property rights. The whole city is a maze of blind alleys leading to the various clan holdings. The housing system is in complete contradiction to our contemporary world of Socialism: forecourt, male area, harem. The question is: should the former Mohammedan woman, now liberated from her veil, live, as the new Socialist woman, in a harem? To rebuild this city of feudalism and capitalism is an enormous task. While many cities must be enlarged, extended and have new parts added to them, others must be allowed to shrink in size. We do not have many buildings of steel and concrete. We build just as well and quite solidly with local materials, such as mud, wood, and stone. We have to be very economical as far as materials are concerned. Our buildings are unencumbered by specific aesthetic intentions. Each material we use represents a deficit unit. Even straw is considered a deficit material. In this sense architecture becomes pure scientific construction. Twelve hundred scientists work in the Institute of Building Sciences for the Testing of Building Materials. We even abandon buildings that have been started and whose foundations have been finished, simply because waste of materials has to be avoided at all costs. An example of this is the building of the Centrosoyus (designed by Le Corbusier). At the moment we lack the capabability to carry out such projects. They are beyond the scope of the present Five-Year Plan. We abandon such unfinished projects, like a cake half eaten, so we can have our daily bread.

Let me say a few words about work speed. It takes four weeks to obtain a site for a project planned today. The House of Soviets, in contrast to the many-angled Palace of Nations in Geneva, was under way within four weeks of its approval. It took four years just to find a site for the Palace of Nations in Geneva. We do not believe in all sorts of zigzags; our buildings are conceived in a straightforward open manner. Insofar as the target date of the Five-Year Plan is conserned, it is only discussed in terms of a reduction to four years. The next four five-year plans have already been prepared.

The function of the artist has changed accordingly. He is obliged to contribute as a member of a collective. He cooperates by painting or by redesigning whole spaces. His work is being included naturally in the normal life of the city. Substance is everything, form is secondary. It is impossible for an artist to run out of inspiration in such a process.

Now to the question of housing! Before the Revolution, Moscow had 1.6 million inhabitants; at the present time this figure is around 2.8 millions. The per capita dwelling area in Moscow is 4.5 square meters (as compared to approximately 12 square meters in Western countries). However, there is a tendency to ignore the square meters devoted to cultural and collective life. As a rule, comparisons are made on the basis of the strictly personal individual living areas in the West. Still, we hope to increase living areas to 7 square meters per capita. Furthermore, around the fringes of Moscow, satellite towns are being built such as Optigozorsk and Mostrikotash, which house the workers of the glass and knitted-goods industries. These are now 30 percent complete.

Outside the Soviet Union much has been said about people queuing up for everything. People do indeed queue up in Moscow, for example, in front of a department store when a large factory happens to close down for a day. People also queue up for movies, as happened when the film *The Road to Living* was being shown. For months it ran uninterruptedly from noon until late at night every day of the week in the largest theaters of Moscow. The largest queue of all, often 5000 meters long, may be found on Red Square in front of Lenin's Tomb, a sacred place to all proletarians of the Soviet Union.

The practical realization of brilliant economic planning in the USSR is only possible because all means of production are in the hands the proletariat, and this is also the reason why unemployment, prostitution, and all the other evils of the capitalist system have been liquidated.

The woman is a comrade in work, in contrast to Parisian women, who spend their time in long discussions on whether the pajama should be considered proper evening attire or not. Our women thing it more important to consider the question of wearing the uniform of the Komsomol. Here I have for the first time been able to observe Socialism as a working system rather than as a figment of the imagination. All our Western upbringing is based on the premise that one and all must participate in the struggle of everybody against everybody else. So far this has been the most characteristic feature of our position. In this connection it is significant that our banks have been designed in the form of temples. The new Russian architecture is the result of a collective will and has not developed according to the wishes of some individual group. Our architecture has the features of collectivism, combined with American functionalism, Leninistic science, and revolutionary flexibility.

Hans Schmidt: The Soviet Union and Modern Architecture*

The outcome of the competition for the Palace of the Soviets has filled all radical architects in the West with indignation and disbelief. We have no intention of using this occasion to mollify their outrage; on the contrary, it is incumbent upon us to inform the reader in the same breath that this decision was neither accidental nor an isolated occurrence. In fact, a limited competition among ten Soviet architects has been held since and has yielded similar results. At the same time, however, we do consider it our duty to give our Western colleagues a more objective picture of the architectural situation in the Soviet Union and to put into perspective those matters that have been misunderstood and distorted by overexposure and sensation-seeking publicity. In our case, the attempt to be objective reflects the desire to look at modern architecture not simply as a completed phenomenon, but as a process intimately connected to all the social, political, and technical manifestations of a whole culture.

Let us first attempt briefly to trace developments as far as the West is concerned. The present situation of modern architecture in the West has come about as the result of a long struggle, with many interacting and mutually interdependent movements often appearing to be countermanding each other, as for example the Arts and Crafts Movement in England, the Dutch Rationalist Movement (Berlage), the Art Nouveau Movement, the Fin de Siècle Movement, etc. The bourgeoisie of the nineteenth century, which after the French Revolution had at first decided to take over the styles bequeathed by feudalism, later attempted by movements such as those mentioned to evolve their own cultural forms in architecture as well as in other fields of artistic endeavor. It is significant to note that all these early attempts had one thing in common: they all tried to find their outlets within the context of high capitalism. As a result of this we had a revival of the Arts and Crafts Movement, the negation of the metropolis, the embracing of social ideas, i.e., garden cities for the workers, etc. Under the influence of technical developments in the last phase of capitalism, and as a result of rationalization and standardization, the real program of modern architecture eventually came into existence, demanding absolute unity between art form and technical form, both firmly rooted in developed capitalist technology. Even here,

* From: *Die Neue Stadt*, VI–VII, Frankfurt/M. 1932, pp. 146–48.

social ideas crept in, such as the notion that prosperity for all could be solved simply by harnessing capitalism to modern technology. The realization that this was not necessarily the case had as its consequence the eventual decision by the left wing of modern architecture to embrace the idea of Socialism.

What then, is the situation in the Soviet Union? The first thing to be established is the fact that there was hardly any participation on the part of tsarist Russia in any of the movements preceding modern architecture. In contrast to the West, the old Russia had neither a superior working class nor a prosperous middle class. An unbridgeable chasm existed between the living standard of the workers and that of the merchants and officials. Unlike their Western colleagues, the Russian architects had no opportunity to acquire new skills by dealing with the problem of the working class dwelling or the middle class house. The victory of the October Revolution brought to the forefront a number of young architects who identified with the aims of the Revolution. Taking up the cudgel in the fight with the older generation of architects they apparently were bringing about the triumph of modern architecture. At a time when relatively very little construction could actually be realized in the Soviet Union, this young and technically inexperienced generation devoted all its energies to utopian projects, in many cases outstripping the real situation of revolutionary development by decades. What was missing, however, was a realistic base for this evolution, both in the efforts of the architects and in their effects on the public. The true situation was revealed only after the initiation of the Five-Year Plan, which represented a monumental effort, and which ushered in a period of complete readjustment and maximum exertion. The Five-Year Plan meant that the country suddenly had to face concrete tasks rather than just fancy dreams. In the Soviet Union of today elaborate utopias have consequently lost much of their attraction. First say goes to the well-trained architect and the experienced technician. In the meantime, a great number of old architects have offered their services to the Soviets. It is clear that these people have filled the vacuum created by modern architecture, which was characterized by a lack of both technical and cultural preparation. Modern architecture succumbed.

This defeat was rendered even more poignant in a situation which manifested itself by revealing an important difference between the West on the one hand and the Soviet Union on the other. In the West, the principles of free competition apply up to a certain point even in the field of the arts. In Soviet Russia, however, all ideas are expected to be subordinate to and integrated into the mainstream of the Revolution. As things stand now, modern architecture has gambled away its chance, at least for the time being. Even the broad masses and youth have joined the ranks of the general opposition. What is even worse, though, is the fact that the modern movement in architecture has presently run into a closed ideological front ranged against it.

On ideological grounds, the following objections have been raised in the Soviet Union against modern architecture:

1. The ideas of modern architecture, known in the West under the labels of "constructivism," "functionalism," and "mechanism," are an outgrowth of contemporary capitalism and its rationalized and standardized technology.

2. Modern architecture's renunciation of monumentality and symbolic expression, its disavowal of absolute beauty, and its inability to carry out the artistic and ideological mission of architecture, are an expression of the decline of bourgeois culture.

3. The idealistic-utopian direction of modern architecture (Le Corbusier), together with the ideas of the "left utopians" in politics, represent an attempt to bypass the natural stages leading toward Socialism, and thus are counter-revolutionary in the political sense.

4. It is not the goal of Socialism to destroy the cultural values of the past; quite to the contrary Socialism, in contrast to disintegrating contemporary capitalism, tries to preserve these values and give them continuity.

We must leave it to thinkers more thoroughly trained in Marxism to test the correctness of these theses. Unfortunately, as far as the history of architecture is concerned, and other intellectual areas as well, genuine historical-materialistic investigations are still lacking. Even though our historians are diligently and devotedly exerting themselves to describe each and every last work of art, they never really bother too much to find out why a particular work of art was created at a specific time and no other.

In the absence of a better answer it is preferable to stick to the program that modern architecture has posed for itself. There is no question that the original point of departure of its program is based on the conditions created by modern capitalism. It may even be possible to characterize these ideas as symptoms of the decline of capitalism, but only in the sense that these ideas have already transcended the limits set by capitalism—in which case modern architecture has to content itself with becoming just another new style in a larger fashion market, a style with which most people are already slightly bored anyway. To a large extent the West already has the technical know-how and the cultural background that modern architecture must take for granted before attempting to transform its whole relationship to architecture in general. The Soviet Union has neither the first nor the second, for even the most extraordinary efforts in the areas of industrialization and the cultural revolution have so far been unable to do much more than lay the foundations. Owing to these circumstances, the setback suffered by modern architecture in the Soviet Union is regrettable, but understandable; this of course proves nothing as far as the righteousness of our challenge is concerned. It should therefore surprise no one when the same young architects who for years and *ad nauseam* have aped the manner of Le Corbusier by making beautiful renderings of glass façades and roof gardens on Watman paper, now draw, under the direction of the old architect-masters, façades of classical beauty on the same Watman paper. Was it really all in vain that modern architecture proclaimed—against the violent protestations of all kinds of halfwits—that as far as goals are concerned it can never be a question of style but must be a question of a fundamentally new conception of the problems of architecture as such? Evidently, the Russian architect, faced by an extremely difficult and extensive cultural task will have to be given some time to regain his senses.

Editor's Postscript

As far as the Palace of Soviets is concerned, our readers have no doubt learned from Volume 5 that a second competition was held in the interim. One of its projects was published in the same volume. At the time of going to press the final decision of the jury (which, it is to be hoped, will thoroughly reverse the decision of the first jury) has not been made known to us.

However, it seems to us that the questions raised by Hans Schmidt in his memorable essay, "How Does Contemporary Russia Relate to the Principles of Modern Architecture?" is much more important than the controversy surrounding the aesthetic views of the jury in Moscow. We see no reason to conceal the fact that the new turn of events that has manifested itself not only in the results of the competition for the Palace of Soviets but that may also be recognized in many of the newly completed administrative structures and apartment buildings, must represent a great shock to all those who believed in the essentially social function of modern architecture. We have always considered the suspicions of such people as Schultze-Naumburg, A. von Senger, and others, who consider each flat roof a symbol of Bolshevism, as so much gibberish. Now we are faced by an almost grotesque reversal of the whole situation, which effectively robs these valiant defenders of a "strictly national" and "traditional" building tradition—in reality nothing other than an allusion to French Baroque of the eighteenth century—of their only argument! Unfortunately, regardless of what arguments may be brought forward to defend the new Russian position, it will be impossible for anyone to accept the fact that those principles of modern architecture that are clearly dictated by social considerations are now being rejected as symptoms of a decaying bourgeois culture by the very same Russians who now consider it their mission to reintroduce the means of expression of a flourishing bourgeois culture, some of which may be considered as of definitely asocial origin. The results are obvious: an aping of historical styles and, in each instance, the achievement of the exact opposite of what has usually been demanded by the principles ostensibly guiding the reconstruction of Russia.

Perhaps the whole matter has to be approached differently; it may be necessary to allow Russia some time to wrestle with all these problems which Europe has fortunately left behind, and let the Russians of the future talk the same way about the architecture of the Five-Year Plan as we talk about the early years of our development. And, may we hope with Hans Schmidt that reason will eventually prevail? "A large ship," said Dostoevsky, "needs a deep channel!"

Gantner

Reports from Moscow*

Taut's Return from Moscow

A report has reached us from Moscow that Professor Bruno Taut has suspended his activities on all the big commissions previously given to him, and that he has submitted a request for indefinite leave. He will return to Germany via Japan, where he has been invited by the government. This abrupt suspension of Taut's activities is not devoid of a certain measure of tragedy. In contrast to those Germans who think about their tasks in Soviet Russia only in the sense of offering their technical skills, Taut belongs to the kind of people who consider their planning for the Russian state as an organizational and artistic expression of their ideology. Only recently, important members of the Soviet government, including Stalin himself, decided no longer to subscribe to this particular interpretation of functionalism, but to ask for a return to the architectural forms of the past. During the past year, a number of reports dealing with the deep disappointments of a good many of the German architects who had moved to Russia and relating to these developments have been published (see our reports in volumes 11, 17, 26, 31 of 1932). It may be expected that Ernst May will have more to say about this subject after his return to Germany, and thus supplement the great lecture he gave in the summer of 1931. It is difficult to make a clear assessment of the full extent of these changes, particularly as far as the translation of Bolshevik ideology into architectural form is concerned. It is quite obvious that the whole matter has been further complicated by a number of more or less superficial formal decisions. Still, the discontinuation of Le Corbusier's building, which had stirred so many hopes at the time when it was started, permits us to come to the conclusion that certain fundamental decisions have indeed been made, and that these decisions were certainly not based altogether on financial difficulties (compare with report from Moscow below).

Climate, Style, and Function

Apart from the heap of rubble marking the spot where once stood a proud cathedral (*Bauwelt* 1932, Vol. 12), with nobody having the faintest notion of what will be built in its place, and discounting the unfinished construction of the "stone bridge" between the Kremlin and the Tsikhouse, which was started four years ago but now lies abandoned with only

---

* From: *Bauwelt*, VII, Berlin 1933, p. 172.

the piers finished, and among the other wounds that have become a blighting feature of the urban landscape of the capital in the last years, the Muscovite may now add another eyesore—the construction site of the new administrative complex on outer Miasnitskaia (Meat Street). Originally planned for use by the Centrosoyus (Center of the Food Distribution Companies), it has now, after the break-up of the National Supreme Economic Council, been designated to house the "People's Commissariat for Light Industry" (Narkom-lekh-prom). It was to have been built according to the plans of Le Corbusier, and there was general apprehension—especially among those holding more rationalistic than stylistic views—that a glass palace of questionable use, unsuited to the local climate, was being created. This uneasiness now seems justified, particularly in view of the fact that almost next door is to be found another recent building, completed only a couple of years ago, which at present houses the Ministry of Supply. Apart from the posts and the lintels, the whole façade of this building consists of glass. The design of the façade has created a great number of unprotected peripheral spaces. This forces people to move themselves and their work to the shady side of the building during the summer, while seeking out warm nooks during the winter, provided they manage to survive at all in any one of these offices. The extent to which this affects work efficiency and the possible damage to health, both permanent and temporary, caused by all this, has not been entirely overlooked.

The reinforced concrete skeleton of Le Corbusier's design was left unfinished for two years, and the gloomy formwork with its protruding rusty steel reinforcing was left staring into the sky along the busy street while the people prayed for sanity. This has changed now, and people passing the building on the street notice with amazement that the exterior shell (in order to free the walls, even the columns have been pushed into the interior, true to Dessau fashion) is being filled in with red cut stone (Arctic tuff from the Caucasus), while the upper part of the protruding wing along the future street alignment has begun to look like the stonewall of a refrigeration plant. The smooth stone surfaces of the other walls are pierced by small, square, prison-like openings. It is true that previously published designs of the elevations call for similar stone surfaces in these areas, and thus the horror of glass walls in other parts of the building (which have been temporarily sheathed with plywood to protect the interior work) may yet become reality.

One can only wonder what kind of stylistic accomplishment the finished building will eventually represent.

Anon., Novosibirsk: On the Subject of Discussions Concerning Russian Architecture*

Lively discussions on the subject of the ideological and practical situation of modern architecture in Russia have been carried more and more frequently not only by this publication, but by other German professional journals as well. It is our intention to direct our critical attention only to those projects that have actually been built within the general framework of the first fiver-year period of Soviet industrialization, in conjunction with a look at some of the theoretical guidelines and ideological devices being used by Soviet members of the profession to justify and explain their work.

The following facts strike one's attention: after the Revolution Russia experienced a flowering of constructivism in art; the pure essence of *l'art pour l'art* and, as Hans Schmidt noted in Volume 6/7, this also included architecture. There was an urge to be more European than the Europeans. However, things changed after the proclamation of the "new line," and the whole reversal was later formalized in Stalin's Six Points. One of these points deals with the mobilization and employment of the old technical intelligentsia. To an astonishing degree these people have succeeded in working their way up again. Education is solid again—one learns from the Old Masters. "Do not hold the Masters in contempt." The classics are once more revered; classicism is being justified (Lunacharski); at the same time one does not yet wish to dismiss Le Corbusier, "the poet of constructivism," altogether. And above all, economy and standardization at all costs! They would *like* to do one thing, but *must* do another. The result is general insecurity, particularly since a theoretical leadership has not developed and directives from the state have not been forthcoming.

In the leading architectural journal, *Stroitelstvo Moskvy*, the architect Grechukho indulges in polemics against rowhouse development in the characteristic manner of dark eclecticism, coupled with an apparent lack of theoretical assurance in the vindication of his thesis. After describing "the monotonous repetition of architecturally unattractive units, all oriented the same way, and spaced at precisely calculated intervals, without consideration of topography and site . . ." as "barracklike" and "boring," the author informs us in addition that cities planned in this manner "resemble settlements built by the bour-

---

* From: *Die Neue Stadt*, XII, Frankfurt/M. 1933, pp. 270–71.

geoisie abroad for its workers." First of all it should be made clear that in the past it was only on the rarest of occasions that workers ever had a chance to live in the foreign settlements alluded to, never mind the present. Secondly, we would like to suggest that the architect Grechukho take a good look at one of these "monotonous" settlements in other countries, or even better, live in one for a while. Finally, the capitalist origin of certain architectural principles does not necessarily preclude their functional usefulness. It may be noted in this connection that Russia is using the same transportation facilities for its workers, such as roads and subways, as the capitalists. In order to be correct, the question ought to be phrased in a different way, i.e., "can a dwelling become a 'machine for dwelling'?" Mr. Grechukho dismisses all this with the old homily that "architecture, after all, is not only a science, but also (!) an art." It is not that easy to dismiss an idea, particularly if it symbolizes a whole program.

Having duly noted the author's rejection of the capitalist form of cities, we read further that "this does not mean that all the features of old cities are necessarily bad and not worthy of being incorporated into our new city plans. There have always been talented builders, capable of producing incomparable compositions (!) for cities and parks that fill us with astonishment (!) even today." So far, so good! However, the things that fill Grechukho with astonishment in these compositions are revealed to us only at the end of the article in his six postulates:

1. He rejects the "preconceived stereotype solutions of the German group of architects and the Ginsburg Group."

   Unfortunately, such stereotype solutions do not exist. What does exist is a general plan for the development of Magnitogorsk by May, and another one for Kuznetsk by Schwagenscheidt. Strictly speaking this is really not quite the whole story, but only its most important part. Evidently the author is looking for something more, some kind of *point de vue*, i.e., "compositions." According to his view, vegetation, water, and topology "must be arranged by the urbanist in the same way as a theater tableau is arranged by the stage designer."

2. Standardization is "not to be repeated *ad nauseam*." Standardization of elements, yes, but under no circumstances standardization of the whole . . .. He is skeptical of norms, "because they have not yet been sufficiently tested." The latter is unfortunately the case, but really only a question of time. Inasmuch as such skepticism

pretends to be based on principle, it flies in the face of all systematic work as such.

Now comes a cheap recipe for classicism:

3. Do not panic or be afraid if something is designed to resemble the good old (!) styles, even if these old concepts should fall into the category of classical solutions.

4. "... do not ignore purely artistic and decorative techniques...."

5. "Return sculpture to architecture, which has for centuries been its close companion."

And to make it quite clear, in the best manner of the "École des Beaux Arts," he adds:

6. "Do not be afraid of the classical concepts of axial and symmetrical composition. The latter applies especially to planning."

One would have expected such dark eclecticism to have been abandoned a long time ago and left to be espoused by its sundry devotees and stalwart adulators, except for the fact that the above list of principles —insofar as this sampling can be dignified by the term principles— has now been elevated to the rank of political postulates in Russia.

In Volume 5/6 of *Die Neue Stadt*, Hans Schmidt has formulated much more succinctly certain objections to the tenets of modern architecture, and it is these that must be taken much more seriously. Among them, the third one ought to be studied very carefully. It deals with the so-called left utopians among modern architects (Le Corbusier), who have been trying to leapfrog all the intermediary stages of normal evolution. Here lies the real source of the danger, for any postulate that demands the subordination of all creative architectural efforts to a general party line *may*—and we emphasize *may*—condemn any bold attempt to push developments to the limits of their technical possibilities as "counter-revolutionary." At the same time it would be interesting to have the apologists of classicism reveal to us the secret of to what degree a symmetry-loving architecture made beautiful by "culture" is more Socialistic than a "house on pylons" by Le Corbusier.

In reality, the rejection of the "monotonous" forms of functionalism in architecture is based on a completely different line of reasoning: poor quality of construction. A construction force, whose members only a few years ago roamed the steppe like nomads or who at best lived the life of peasants in the villages, quite frequently up to 75 percent of them women, often including girls in their twenties, will inevitably turn modern functionalism into something crudely primitive. This has been openly admitted by our Russian colleagues in the profession. This is also the reason for reverting to round staircases, bulls' eyes, cornices, and ultimately "related sculpture" and classical symmetry: involvement with form rather than quality. One might even be tempted to concede that sculptural monumentality, which by now has lost its meaning in the West, has in Russia regained some of its lost meaning in the political sense, but surely not as an ornament of architecture.

If the Russians persist in trying to go their own way politically and artistically, then they are only doing what the whole world expected them to do anyway. At the same time it remains a mystery why it should be permissible to use the cultural forms of expression from the Golden Age of the bourgeoisie, such as classicism in architecture, romantic music, and Strauss waltzes, but not the new functionalism in architecture, or new dance music. As far as the suitability of the functional principles developed in the West is concerned, the Russians have good reason to be cautious. The accomplishments of Gropius, May, Taut, and others may be summed up as follows: a city form expressing an economically and spiritually fragmented bourgeois society of single individuals. In contrast to earlier stages of conservative bourgeois development, their city plans reflect the life style of the liberal middle classes, with a tendency toward communal and cooperative community centralization of various life functions. What they did not find, could not find, and therefore could not bring to Russia, was a master plan that would have focused the political-educational purposes of the mass movements (for example, the movements of May 1, May 2, and October 8). Their "garden cities," "satellite cities," and "peripheral cities" are nothing more—but also nothing less—than systematic aggregations of roughly equal dwelling units designed according to optimal norms of hygiene and light. To each adult his own room and the maximum of light and quiet or, even better, to be left alone in peace. That in itself is a great achievement and should help to enrich the vocabulary of Soviet-Russian city planning. All this is necessary, but not sufficient. The political and propagandistic significance of a city plan, especially with reference to its squares and civic centers, has so far scarcely been recognized. Similarly it is not enough to view the integration of communal buildings, clubs, bachelors' homes, community centers, kindergartens, and dining halls with their respective districts merely as a sort of functional appendix, for their symbolic significance as politically exemplary focal points is equally important. Insofar as these "supplementary buildings" are known at all in the West, they represent only an anticipatory stage in the over-all context of housing, based on completely different social considerations, while in Russia they tend to take on the function of political showpieces, notwithstanding the fact that at present they represent only 25 percent of the total housing construction. The communal dwelling that represents one of the most advanced and pure examples of its type, and that at the present is still relatively rare, is usually under the patronage of a large factory, which clearly illustrates the relevance of the public character of this type of building. In conclusion, it should be pointed out that in a country where the workers are the masters of their own factories, this new relationship between factory and dwelling should also be reflected in the plan of the city. At any rate, none of these questions has been answered by the Russians, much less by the German architects working in Russia. In this respect, the opportunities of Russian planning clearly lie in the direction of a meaningful expansion of the rowhouse concept developed in the West, and it is precisely for this reason that one expects more from the Russians than mere historical plagiarism. To ignore Western city planning simply for the reason that it "resembles settlements built by the capitalists for their workers" is silly and primitive. Such political arrogance convinces no one and leads nowhere.

There is no proof to what extent the views and theories presently being circulated in Russia have been initiated or approved by high Soviet officials or competent theoreticians. An official clarification of these questions may be expected during the forthcoming International Congress in Moscow. Without doubt there will be many a surprise and no shortage of criticism on both sides.

Index

May, Ernst
  planning of Magnitogorsk, 176,
  178–179, 187, 226
  in Russia, 173–175
Mayakovsky, 12
Melnikov, K., 12
Meyer, Hannes, 213
Meyerhold, 12, 168
Mies van der Rohe, Ludwig, 15,
  135
Miliutin, 191–192, 199
Mir-Isskustva (World of Art),
  20
Moholy-Nagy, Laszlo, 15
Mondrian, Piet, 144
Mongol invasions, 16–17
Monument to the Third Inter-
  national, 29, 147
Moscow, 17–18, 50, 158, 164,
  172, 175, 202, 221, 223
  Academy of Arts, 135
  central archives, 164
  Centrosoyus; see Le Corbusier
  dissolution plans for, 180
  expansion of, 175
  housing shortage in, 184, 216
  Lissitzky in, 135–136
  Main Telegraph Building, 172
  Place of the Soviets, 172
  satellite cities proposal for, 193,
  216
  sky-hook, 56
Mossoviet, 37
Motion pictures, 148
Multi-media, 135–137, 148
MVTU, Moscow Institute of
  Architecture, 158

NARKOMPROS (Commissariat
  of the People's Education), 21
National Economic Council, 208
Nevski Pickwickians, 20
New Economic Policy (NEP), 21
Nikolski, A., 52

Novosibirsk, 5, 13, 15, 50–51,
  180, 193
  planning of, 180–183

Objectivism, 22
October Revolution, 16, 18–19,
  22, 27, 68, 159, 168, 219
  architectural tasks of, 22, 158
  expropriations after, 159–161
  living conditions after, 156
  radical artist and, 28
  urban policies after, 163
Office buildings, 50, 62
  Central Consumer Cooperatives,
  53
  Central Industrial Administra-
  tion, 52
  government, in Alma Ata, 52
  Novosibirsk, 5
  Palace of Industry in Kharkov,
  51
  sky-hook. See Lissitzky; pro-
  jects
  State Trade Center, Kharkov, 51
Okhitovich, 179
Olearius, A., 35
OSA, 158
Oud, 15
Painting, 28, 140, 149–150
  as a transfer point for archi-
  tecture, 29, 133
Palace of Nations (Geneva), 216
Palace of Soviets; see Le Corbusier
Palaces of Labor; see Clubs
Pan-Slavists, 20
Paris Worlds Fair (1925), 32
Peredvizhniki (Wanderers), 20, 22
Pasternak (architect), 38
Perspective; see Space; perspective
Peter I (1682–1725), 18, 20
Petrograd Free Studios; see SVO-
  MAS
Physculture; see Sports
Picasso, 144

239